DELIVERANCE PRAYER FOR TEENAGE SON

"Anointing & Power for Family Deliverance"

Book 3

TIMOTHY ATUNNISE

Glovim Publishing House
Atlanta, Georgia

DELIVERANCE PRAYER FOR TEENAGE SON

Copyright © 2024 by Timothy Atunnise

All rights reserved. No part of this book may be reproduced, copied, stored or transmitted in any form or by any means – graphic, electronic, or mechanical, including photocopying, recording, or information storage and retrieval systems without the prior written permission of Glovim Publishing House except where permitted by law.

Glovim Publishing House
1078 Citizens Pkwy
Suite A
Morrow, Georgia 30260

glovimbooks@gmail.com
www.glovimonline.org

Printed in the United States of America

Table of Contents

Introduction 7

Understanding the Need for Deliverance 11

Prayers for Protection 42

Breaking the Chains of Addiction 71

Healing from Emotional Wounds & Trauma 100

Prayers for Godly Character Development 131

Overcoming the Spirit of Rebellion & Disobedience 161

Sustaining Your Son's Deliverance 193

Other bestselling books from the author 224

Introduction

In the quiet hours of the night, as the world sleeps and the house falls silent, a mother's heart remains restless. Her thoughts are filled with concerns for her teenage son — the boy she once cradled in her arms, who is now navigating the tumultuous waters of adolescence. His world is complex, filled with new challenges and unseen battles that test his spirit, tempt his heart, and tug at his soul. She sees the struggles, the subtle changes in his demeanor, the influence of a culture that is increasingly alien to the values she has nurtured within him. The weight of worry rests heavily on her shoulders, and she knows, deep down, that these are not just natural growing pains. They are spiritual battles — battles that require a weapon far greater than anything the world can offer.

This book, Deliverance Prayers for Your Teenage Son, is born from that very place of a parent's concern and a Christian's calling. As parents, we want to protect our children from every harm, shield them from every pain, and guard them against every threat. Yet, we find ourselves powerless against the unseen forces that wage war against their souls. We are witnessing an unprecedented assault on the hearts and minds of our youth — a generation under siege by the spirit of this age. From the lure of addiction to the snare of social media, from the rise of anxiety and depression to the rebellion and disobedience that seem to permeate our homes, our sons are under attack. The enemy is relentless, and his strategies are cunning. But we, as parents, have a divine weapon that is mightier than any scheme of darkness: prayer.

Prayer is not a last resort; it is our first line of defense. It is the lifeline that connects us to the power and presence of the Almighty God. Through prayer, we can stand in the gap for our sons, interceding on their behalf, pleading for their protection, deliverance, and spiritual growth. We can declare the promises of God over their lives, break the chains of addiction and bondage, and release them into their God-ordained destinies. Our prayers are a force of divine intervention, calling down the power of heaven to confront the powers of darkness. This is the call of every parent who desires not just to see their child grow up, but to see them grow up in the Lord.

But how do we pray effectively for our teenage sons in a world that is increasingly hostile to their faith? How do we address the specific issues they face, the struggles they endure, and the fears they carry? How do we speak words of life into their situations, knowing that our prayers have the power to shape their futures? This book is designed to guide you through these very questions. It is a resource, a companion, and a manual for spiritual warfare tailored to the unique needs of teenage boys.

In these pages, you will find prayers that address the deepest concerns of a parent's heart — prayers for protection, for deliverance from addiction, for healing from emotional wounds, and for the cultivation of godly character. You will discover how to pray with authority, using the Word of

God as your weapon and the Holy Spirit as your guide. You will learn how to break the strongholds that the enemy has tried to erect in your son's life and how to release him into the freedom that Christ has already secured on the cross. You will be encouraged to persevere in prayer, even when the results are not immediate, knowing that God is faithful and that He hears the cries of a parent's heart.

We must remember that our sons are not only our children; they are also the sons of God. He loves them with an everlasting love, a love that is stronger than any force of darkness and deeper than any ocean of despair. He knows every hair on their heads, every fear in their hearts, and every step on their path. As we pray, we align ourselves with His perfect will for their lives, surrendering our desires to His divine plans, and trusting that He who began a good work in them will be faithful to complete it.

This journey will not always be easy. There will be moments when you feel overwhelmed by the enormity of the task or discouraged by the lack of visible change. But take heart. Your prayers are seeds sown in faith, watered by tears, and nurtured by hope. They will bear fruit in due season. The enemy may try to convince you that your prayers are powerless, that your son is too far gone, or that the battle is already lost. But remember this: the enemy is a liar, and his defeat is already written. Jesus Christ has already won the victory, and it is His name that you will call upon as you intercede for your son.

Let this book be a source of strength and encouragement to you. Let it be a reminder that you are not alone in this battle and that the God of all creation is fighting alongside you. As you read these prayers, know that you are engaging in a holy battle, one that will shape not only your son's future but also his eternity. You are stepping onto the battlefield with the armor of God, armed with His Word, covered by His blood, and empowered by His Spirit.

May this book inspire you to pray with boldness, with faith, and with the assurance that the One who holds your son's life in His hands is both mighty to save and faithful to deliver. This is your calling, this is your weapon, and this is your victory.

Chapter 1

Understanding the Need for Deliverance

Recognizing Spiritual Warfare in Your Son's Life

Spiritual warfare is an often-overlooked reality in the lives of many Christians, particularly when it comes to our children. As parents, we may find ourselves preoccupied with our sons' physical, emotional, and academic well-being, but neglect to address the spiritual battles they face daily. To recognize spiritual warfare in your teenage son's life, you must first understand the unseen forces at play and how they can influence and shape his behavior, thoughts, and emotions.

Understanding the Reality of Spiritual Warfare

The Bible makes it abundantly clear that we live in a world that is both physical and spiritual. Ephesians 6:12 states, "For we wrestle not against flesh and blood, but against principalities, against powers, against the rulers of the darkness of this world, against spiritual wickedness in high places." This scripture reminds us that our struggles are not merely with human challenges but with spiritual forces that seek to undermine God's purpose for our lives—and, importantly, the lives of our children.

For your teenage son, the battlefield is often his mind, emotions, and identity. The enemy is keenly aware of the significance of the teenage years—this critical period of development where identity, beliefs, and life direction are formed. During these years, the enemy works tirelessly to sow seeds of doubt, rebellion, fear, and confusion. If we fail to recognize these spiritual attacks, we leave our sons vulnerable to the schemes of the devil.

Signs of Spiritual Warfare in Your Teenage Son's Life

- Sudden and Unexplained Changes in Behavior: Spiritual attacks often manifest as sudden, unexplained shifts in behavior. Your son, who was once joyful, obedient, and respectful, may become sullen, rebellious, or withdrawn. He may start to exhibit anger outbursts, disrespect toward authority, or a marked change in his demeanor that seems to come out of nowhere. These changes are not just a 'phase' but may signal an underlying spiritual battle.

- Increased Interest in Dark or Ungodly Activities: Another sign of spiritual warfare is an increased interest in activities that are contrary to God's will. This could include fascination with the occult, horror movies, violent video games, or any form of media that glorifies darkness. The enemy seeks to lure young minds into a fascination with the forbidden, subtly pulling them away from the light of God.

- Emotional Instability and Mental Oppression: If your son is struggling with severe anxiety, depression, or inexplicable fear, he may be under spiritual attack. The enemy targets our minds with lies, seeking to cripple us with negative thoughts and feelings. The Bible calls Satan "the father of lies" (John 8:44), and his aim is to make your son believe falsehoods about himself, God, and the world around him.

- Isolation and Withdrawal from Godly Influence: When spiritual warfare is at its peak, you may notice your son withdrawing from his faith community, avoiding church, or becoming less interested in spiritual matters. He may resist prayer, Bible study, or any discussion about God. This is a common tactic of the enemy—to isolate so he can destroy. Satan knows that a lone believer is easier to attack than one who is surrounded by a strong support system.

- Nightmares and Disturbed Sleep Patterns: Spiritual warfare often manifests through physical symptoms, such as nightmares, night terrors, or disturbed sleep patterns. If your son is frequently waking up in fear, experiencing night sweats, or expressing a fear of the dark or being alone at night, these could be signs of a spiritual attack in the form of oppression or harassment from demonic forces.

How to Recognize the Source of the Battle

Recognizing spiritual warfare requires spiritual discernment. This is not simply about identifying surface-level symptoms but understanding the deeper spiritual implications behind them. James 1:5 encourages us to seek wisdom from God: "If any of you lacks wisdom, let him ask of God, who gives to all liberally and without reproach, and it will be given to him." Begin by praying for wisdom and discernment. Ask God to open your spiritual eyes to see the root causes of the issues your son is facing.

Ask yourself critical questions: Are these behaviors consistent with a spiritual battle? Do they align with any known patterns of spiritual attack described in Scripture? Do they defy natural explanation or resist normal parental interventions? Remember, the enemy often camouflages his attacks to make them appear as ordinary life issues. However, when viewed through the lens of spiritual discernment, these patterns become evident.

Spiritual Warfare and the Role of the Parent

As a parent, you are called to be the spiritual watchman over your son's life. In Ezekiel 3:17, God speaks to the prophet saying, "Son of man, I have made you a watchman for the house of Israel; therefore hear a word from My mouth, and give them warning from Me." Similarly, you are called to stand in the gap for your son, to intercede on his behalf, and to wage war in the spiritual realm.

Your role as a parent is to create an environment of spiritual safety, where your son feels protected, loved, and understood. This involves not only prayer but also active engagement in his life. Engage in open and honest conversations about what he is experiencing, listening without judgment, and providing biblical counsel when necessary. Encourage him to express his fears, doubts, and anxieties so that you can pray specifically against the strongholds the enemy may be trying to build.

Strategies for Spiritual Discernment and Intervention

- Pray for the Gift of Discernment: Spiritual discernment is a gift from the Holy Spirit (1 Corinthians 12:10). Regularly ask God to sharpen your ability to discern what is happening in your son's life. Pray specifically that the Holy Spirit will reveal the schemes of the enemy and expose any hidden areas where the enemy may have a foothold.

- Speak the Word of God Boldly: Hebrews 4:12 reminds us that "the word of God is alive and active, sharper than any double-edged sword." Use scripture to speak life over your son. Declare God's promises and truths over him daily. Remind him of his identity in Christ and the authority he has over the enemy.

- Anoint Your Home and Son with Oil: Use anointing oil as a symbol of the Holy Spirit's presence and protection. Pray over your son and your home, anointing doors and windows while declaring God's authority and protection. This is a physical act that represents a spiritual reality.

- Encourage Spiritual Habits: Encourage your son to engage in daily spiritual practices like prayer, Bible reading, and worship. These habits will build his spiritual resilience and help him recognize and resist the enemy's tactics.

- Surround Him with Godly Influence: Help your son build relationships with godly mentors, peers, and leaders who can provide spiritual support and encouragement. The enemy's attacks are weakened when a young person is surrounded by a strong, faith-filled community.

Recognizing spiritual warfare in your teenage son's life is not about fear but empowerment. It's about understanding the enemy's tactics, discerning the signs, and taking proactive steps to intercede on his behalf. As you engage in this spiritual battle, remember that you are not alone. God is with you, and He has equipped you with everything you need to stand firm and claim victory over the forces of darkness. Your role is crucial, and your prayers are powerful. As James 5:16 says, "The effective, fervent prayer of a righteous man avails much." Be bold, be vigilant, and trust in God's unfailing power to deliver your son from every scheme of the enemy.

Common Signs of Spiritual Oppression in Teenagers

Spiritual oppression is a reality that many parents may not immediately recognize in their teenage sons. It can manifest in various ways, some subtle and some glaringly obvious. Understanding these signs is the first step in waging effective spiritual warfare on behalf of your son.

1. Recognizing the Shift: Changes in Behavior and Attitude

One of the most telling signs of spiritual oppression is a sudden, unexplained change in your son's behavior and attitude. This could range from increased anger, irritability, and mood swings to withdrawal from family and friends. You might notice that your son, once full of joy and optimism, is now constantly in a state of despair or indifference. He may start displaying disrespect toward authority figures, including you, his teachers, and even spiritual leaders.

These changes are not merely hormonal or a "phase" that all teenagers go through; they may indicate a deeper, spiritual struggle. The enemy often attacks young people by sowing seeds of rebellion and disobedience. Ephesians 6:12 reminds us that "our struggle is not against flesh and blood, but against the rulers, against the authorities, against the powers of this dark world and against the spiritual forces of evil in the heavenly realms." When you observe these shifts, recognize them as potential spiritual battles that require intercessory prayer and spiritual insight.

2. Obsession with Darkness: Involvement in Occultic or Sinful Practices

Another significant sign of spiritual oppression is a newfound fascination or obsession with dark, occultic, or sinful practices. This may manifest as an interest in witchcraft, tarot cards, Ouija boards, dark-themed video games, horror movies, or music with violent or blasphemous lyrics. Your son may start exploring alternative spiritual practices that contradict the teachings of the Bible, such as astrology, crystals, or New Age ideologies.

It is crucial to understand that the enemy uses these mediums to establish a foothold in the lives of young people. Proverbs 4:23 advises, "Above all else, guard your heart, for everything you do flows from it." If your son is becoming desensitized to darkness, it may be a sign that his spiritual guard has been compromised. The enemy is seeking to dull his spiritual senses, making him more susceptible to further spiritual attack. As a parent, it's essential to confront this behavior with love and biblical truth, engaging in prayer to break the enemy's grip on his heart and mind.

3. Emotional and Mental Turmoil: Anxiety, Depression, and Hopelessness

While emotional and mental struggles like anxiety and depression can have multiple causes, spiritual oppression can often amplify these conditions. When your son is under spiritual attack, he may begin to experience overwhelming feelings of fear, worry, sadness, and hopelessness. These emotions can lead to panic attacks, nightmares, insomnia, or an inability to concentrate on schoolwork or daily activities.

Psalm 42:11 says, "Why, my soul, are you downcast? Why so disturbed within me? Put your hope in God, for I will yet praise him, my Savior and my God." This verse acknowledges that our souls can indeed be cast down and disturbed. Still, it points to the remedy: placing hope in God. As a parent, it is crucial to recognize that these symptoms may not just be psychological but could be a sign of a deeper spiritual battle. Pray fervently for the peace of Christ to guard your son's heart and mind (Philippians 4:7), and speak God's truth into his life to counter the lies of the enemy.

4. Social Isolation: Withdrawal from Family, Church, and Friends

One of the enemy's strategies in spiritual warfare is to isolate his target. If your son suddenly withdraws from his family, avoids church activities, or distances himself from his friends, it may be a sign that he is under spiritual attack. The enemy knows that there is strength in fellowship and unity; he seeks to cut off your son from his spiritual support system.

Hebrews 10:25 encourages believers not to give up meeting together, "as some are in the habit of doing, but encouraging one another—and all the more as you see the Day approaching." Isolation makes your son more vulnerable to the enemy's lies and discouragement. Combat this tactic with a prayer strategy that includes asking the Holy Spirit to draw your son back into community, open his heart to Godly counsel, and restore his desire for fellowship.

5. Spiritual Apathy: A Loss of Interest in God, Prayer, and Scripture

Perhaps the most alarming sign of spiritual oppression is spiritual apathy—a loss of interest in God, prayer, and Scripture. Your son may have once shown enthusiasm for church activities, Bible study, or personal prayer time, but now he seems indifferent or even hostile toward these practices. He may express doubt about his faith, question God's goodness, or reject spiritual teachings altogether.

Revelation 3:15-16 warns about lukewarmness: "I know your deeds, that you are neither cold nor hot. I wish you were either one or the other! So, because you are lukewarm—neither hot nor cold—I am about to spit you out of my mouth." This verse underscores the danger of spiritual indifference. If your son is no longer spiritually engaged, it may indicate that he is under attack and that the enemy is trying to steal his zeal for God.

To combat spiritual apathy, pray persistently for the fire of the Holy Spirit to reignite your son's passion for God. Ask God to reveal Himself to your son in a powerful and undeniable way, and to rekindle his first love for Christ (Revelation 2:4-5).

Awakening to the Spiritual Reality

As a parent, you have a significant role to play in discerning these signs of spiritual oppression and acting accordingly. It is essential not to dismiss these changes as mere teenage rebellion or mood swings but to engage in spiritual warfare on behalf of your son. Utilize the authority given to you through Christ (Luke 10:19) and stand firm in prayer, fasting, and the Word of God.

Remember that the goal of the enemy is to destroy your son's future and potential. Still, you have the power to intercede and fight back.

Identifying the Strongholds: Addictions, Anger, and Anxiety

The teenage years are a time of immense change, exploration, and growth. However, they can also be a period marked by significant spiritual vulnerability. Many parents notice changes in their teenage sons—an unexplainable heaviness, withdrawal, sudden anger, or even addictions to substances, technology, or destructive behaviors. These signs may point to more than just the typical struggles of adolescence; they may indicate spiritual strongholds that require deliberate and focused prayer. As Christian parents, it is essential to understand these strongholds and seek God's wisdom and power to help dismantle them.

Understanding Spiritual Strongholds: What Are They?

In Christian terms, a stronghold is more than a mere habit or behavior; it is a fortress built in the mind or spirit, often through repeated sin, trauma, or exposure to negative influences. The Apostle Paul describes strongholds in 2 Corinthians 10:4-5: "The weapons we fight with are not the weapons of the world. On the contrary, they have divine power to demolish strongholds. We demolish arguments and every pretension that sets itself up against the knowledge of God." A stronghold is, therefore, anything that exalts itself in the mind, pretending to be bigger or more powerful than God's truth.

For teenagers, these strongholds can manifest in many forms, such as addictions, uncontrollable anger, and overwhelming anxiety. Let us explore these common strongholds in greater detail, uncovering their spiritual roots and providing a pathway for deliverance through prayer.

Addictions: A Grip That Needs Breaking

Addictions are one of the most pervasive strongholds affecting today's youth. They come in various forms—substance abuse (like alcohol, drugs, or vaping), technology addiction (excessive use of social media, video games, or internet), and even addictive patterns of behavior such as pornography, self-harm, or gambling. These addictions are not merely physical or psychological issues; they have spiritual dimensions that must be addressed through the lens of deliverance.

Addictions are often rooted in a deep spiritual void or a misplaced need for fulfillment that only God can provide. Teenagers may turn to substances or behaviors to numb pain, escape reality, or fill a void in their lives. Yet, the enemy uses these habits to ensnare and bind them in a cycle of bondage. Jesus speaks clearly about this in John 10:10: "The thief comes only to steal and kill and destroy; I have come that they may have life and have it to the full." Addictions rob our children of the abundant life Christ offers and enslave them to destructive patterns.

How to Pray Against Addictions:
- Pray for Revelation: Ask the Holy Spirit to reveal the root cause of your son's addiction. Is it rooted in a past trauma, an unmet emotional need, or a desire for acceptance? Only when the root is exposed can the healing begin.
- Pray for Freedom and Release: Command the spirit of addiction to leave in the name of Jesus. Speak out scriptures that declare freedom, such as Galatians 5:1: "It is for freedom that Christ has set us free. Stand firm, then, and do not let yourselves be burdened again by a yoke of slavery."
- Pray for a Holy Hunger: Replace the unhealthy cravings with a desire for God's presence. Pray for a holy hunger to replace their dependency on substances or behaviors with a longing for spiritual things.

Anger: A Weapon Turned Inward and Outward

Anger is another powerful stronghold that can take root in a teenage boy's heart, leading to devastating consequences if left unchecked. While anger itself is not a sin, as it is a natural human emotion, the Bible warns against letting anger turn into sin or allowing it to control us: "In your anger do not sin: Do not let the sun go down while you are still angry, and do not give the devil a foothold." (Ephesians 4:26-27).

Teenagers often experience anger due to frustrations, unmet expectations, identity struggles, or feeling misunderstood. However, the enemy can manipulate these feelings of anger, using them to establish a stronghold. When anger is harbored, it can manifest as rebellion, violent behavior, self-harm, or deep-seated resentment against parents, peers, or authority figures. It can also lead to feelings of shame or self-condemnation, trapping the teenager in a cycle of anger and guilt.

How to Pray Against Anger:

- Pray for a Spirit of Forgiveness: Anger often stems from unresolved hurt or unforgiveness. Pray for your son to have the strength to forgive those who have wronged him, even himself. Declare Matthew 6:14: "For if you forgive other people when they sin against you, your heavenly Father will also forgive you."
- Pray for Peace and Self-Control: Ask God to flood your son's heart with peace, as promised in Philippians 4:7: "And the peace of God, which transcends all understanding, will guard your hearts and your minds in Christ Jesus." Pray for the fruit of self-control to be evident in his life.
- Pray Against the Spirit of Anger: Take authority over any spirit of anger that has taken root in your son's life. In the name of Jesus, break its power and command it to leave. Use spiritual weapons like praise and worship to break down this stronghold.

Anxiety: The Thief of Peace and Joy

Anxiety is one of the most crippling strongholds affecting teenagers today. With constant pressures from academics, social circles, future expectations, and identity struggles, many young people find themselves overwhelmed by fear, worry, and anxiety. The Bible teaches us that anxiety is a spiritual battle—a weapon used by the enemy to paralyze us with fear and keep us from stepping into our God-given destiny. Jesus commands us not to worry: "Therefore do not worry about tomorrow, for tomorrow will worry about itself. Each day has enough trouble of its own." (Matthew 6:34).

However, anxiety does not disappear simply by ignoring it; it requires a proactive spiritual approach. Anxiety can stem from a lack of trust in God's plans, a desire for control, or a reaction to past trauma. If left unaddressed, it can grow into a stronghold that affects every aspect of a teenager's life, including their physical health, relationships, and spiritual growth.

How to Pray Against Anxiety:
- Pray for a Sound Mind: Declare 2 Timothy 1:7 over your son: "For God has not given us a spirit of fear, but of power and of love and of a sound mind." Pray for the spirit of fear to be replaced with courage, love, and a sound mind.
- Pray for God's Peace: Ask God to fill your son with His perfect peace that transcends understanding. Pray against the spirit of worry and cast all anxieties upon God (1 Peter 5:7).
- Pray for Trust and Surrender: Help your son to trust God's plans over his own fears. Pray that he will learn to surrender his concerns at the feet of Jesus, understanding that God's plans for him are good, as Jeremiah 29:11 promises.

The Power of Focused Prayer

Identifying these strongholds is the first step toward deliverance for your teenage son. As a parent, your prayers have immense power to break chains, destroy strongholds, and release your son into the freedom and purpose God has ordained for him. By understanding the nature of these spiritual battles, and praying specifically and boldly against each one, you align yourself with God's will to set your son free and bring him into His glorious light. Remember, as Jesus declared, "If the Son sets you free, you will be free indeed." (John 8:36). Stand firm, pray without ceasing, and watch as God moves mightily in your son's life.

Understanding Your Role as a Spiritual Guardian

In the spiritual realm, parents hold a unique position as guardians over their children, especially during the turbulent teenage years. This role is not merely a parental duty but a divine calling—a sacred trust given by God to safeguard, nurture, and guide the spiritual development of your son. To understand this role fully, we must delve into the scriptural foundation, embrace the authority given to us by God, and recognize the urgency of the spiritual battle that rages for the soul of your teenage son.

The Scriptural Foundation of Spiritual Guardianship

The Bible clearly articulates the role of parents as spiritual overseers in several key passages. Proverbs 22:6 encourages, "Train up a child in the way he should go, and when he is old, he will not depart from it." This verse signifies more than just teaching; it's about guiding your son into a relationship with God that is built on solid biblical principles. It is a proactive stance, one that requires intentionality and persistence.

Furthermore, Deuteronomy 6:6-7 provides an even deeper insight into the role of parents: "These commandments that I give you today are to be on your hearts. Impress them on your children. Talk about them when you sit at home and when you walk along the road, when you lie down and when you get up." The act of impressing God's Word on your son is not a passive task. It involves consistent communication, prayer, and active demonstration of God's love and truth in everyday life.

Understanding these scriptures is the first step toward embracing your role as a spiritual guardian. You are called to be more than just a provider or protector in the physical sense; you are ordained to be a spiritual warrior, standing in the gap for your son in the spiritual battlefield.

Embracing Your God-Given Authority

As a parent, you have been given authority by God to stand against the powers of darkness on behalf of your son. In Matthew 18:18, Jesus declared, "Truly I tell you, whatever you bind on earth will be bound in heaven, and whatever you loose on earth will be loosed in heaven." This verse is not limited to church leaders or pastors; it is a promise for every believer, including you as a parent.

When you speak God's Word over your son, you are wielding a sword that cuts through the lies of the enemy. When you pray fervently, you are shaking the gates of hell, setting in motion heavenly forces to intervene on your son's behalf. The authority you have as a parent is not based on your strength but on the power of the Holy Spirit dwelling within you (Romans 8:11). You are commissioned to fight for your son's destiny, knowing that God stands with you, empowering you to accomplish His divine will.

The Urgency of the Spiritual Battle for Your Son's Soul

The teenage years are marked by exploration, questioning, and a deep desire for identity and belonging. This season is also a time when the enemy intensifies his attacks, knowing that the choices made during these formative years can shape your son's destiny. Ephesians 6:12 reminds us, "For we do not wrestle against flesh and blood, but against principalities, against powers, against the rulers of the darkness of this age, against spiritual hosts of wickedness in the heavenly places."

The urgency of your role as a spiritual guardian is underscored by the reality of this battle. Your teenage son is not merely facing societal pressures, peer influences, or hormonal changes; he is in a spiritual fight against forces that seek to steal his joy, kill his purpose, and destroy his future (John 10:10). As his parent, you are called to be vigilant, recognizing that the enemy's tactics are subtle but relentless—ranging from temptations of addiction and immorality to feelings of worthlessness and despair.

Your response must be equally relentless. You must pray with boldness and authority, declaring God's promises over your son. You must teach him to wear the full armor of God (Ephesians 6:13-17), equipping him with the helmet of salvation, the breastplate of righteousness, the belt of truth, and the sword of the Spirit. As a spiritual guardian, you are also responsible for modeling this armor yourself, showing him what it means to stand firm in faith amidst trials.

Becoming a Watchman: Standing on the Spiritual Wall

In Ezekiel 33:7, God calls His servant to be a watchman: "Son of man, I have made you a watchman for the house of Israel; therefore, hear a word from My mouth, and give them warning from Me." Similarly, as a parent, you are a watchman over your son's life. A watchman stands on the wall, alert and vigilant, ready to sound the alarm at the first sign of danger.

You must be spiritually attuned to the Holy Spirit, discerning when your son is under attack. This means praying without ceasing (1 Thessalonians 5:17), seeking God's wisdom for every situation, and being quick to act when you sense the enemy's influence. It involves creating a spiritual environment in your home where God's presence is felt, where prayer and worship are as natural as breathing, and where your son feels safe, loved, and spiritually fed.

Reclaiming Your Son's Destiny Through Strategic Prayer

Your prayers have the power to change the course of your son's life. As a spiritual guardian, you are called to intercede for him strategically. This is not about offering generic prayers but specific, targeted ones that address his unique struggles and needs. Speak life over him daily. Pray for his mind, that he would think on things that are pure, lovely, and praiseworthy (Philippians 4:8). Pray for his heart, that he would have a heart of flesh and not stone (Ezekiel 36:26). Pray for his spirit, that he would be sensitive to God's voice and obedient to His leading.

Every time you pray, you are sowing seeds into his future. These seeds may not sprout immediately, but they will grow in God's perfect timing. You may not see the results right away, but remember, God is faithful to His promises (2 Corinthians 1:20). Your role is to continue standing in faith, knowing that your labor in the Lord is not in vain (1 Corinthians 15:58).

A Call to Action

Understanding your role as a spiritual guardian is understanding that you are engaged in a high-stakes spiritual battle for your son's soul. It requires dedication, discernment, and determination to see him set free from every chain and hindrance. The enemy does not take breaks, and neither should you. Be bold, be vigilant, and never underestimate the power of a praying parent. Remember, God is on your side, and He is fighting with you. Your son's deliverance is not just possible; it is promised. Stand firm, take up your authority, and declare, "As for me and my house, we will serve the Lord" (Joshua 24:15).

Preparing Spiritually for the Journey Ahead

Preparing spiritually for the journey of deliverance for your teenage son is more than just a routine of prayers or a checklist of activities. It is a sacred calling, a divine assignment that requires unwavering faith, steadfast commitment, and a heart fully surrendered to God's will. To navigate this journey, you must recognize that deliverance is not a one-time event but a continuous process that demands spiritual resilience and discernment.

Understanding the Foundation: Building on the Rock of Christ

Before engaging in the spiritual battle for your son's deliverance, it is essential to establish a firm foundation in Christ. Jesus taught in Matthew 7:24-27 about the importance of building on the rock. The rock represents an unshakeable faith in God's Word, a life grounded in His truth. As a parent, your spiritual preparation begins with examining your own walk with God. Are you building on a solid foundation, or are there cracks that need attention?

This journey will test your faith and expose the weaknesses in your spiritual armor. It will challenge your endurance, your patience, and your understanding of God's promises. Therefore, it is crucial to immerse yourself in the Word of God, allowing it to penetrate every part of your life. Memorize scriptures that speak of God's power, His faithfulness, and His deliverance. Scriptures like Isaiah 54:17, "No weapon formed against you shall prosper," and 2 Corinthians 10:4, "The weapons of our warfare are not carnal, but mighty through God to the pulling down of strongholds," should be the anchor of your prayers.

Cultivating a Spirit of Worship: Ushering in God's Presence

Worship is a powerful weapon in spiritual warfare. It invites the presence of God and disarms the enemy. The story of King Jehoshaphat in 2 Chronicles 20 is a vivid example of how worship can turn the tide in a battle. Faced with a formidable enemy, Jehoshaphat appointed singers to go before the army, singing, "Give thanks to the Lord, for His love endures forever." As they began to sing and praise, the Lord set ambushes against their enemies.

Likewise, as you prepare for this journey, make worship a priority. Create an atmosphere of praise in your home. Let worship music fill your space, and make time each day to worship God personally and corporately with your family. Worship softens hardened hearts, breaks down spiritual barriers, and brings clarity and peace amid confusion. It reminds you of

God's greatness and power, reinforcing your confidence in His ability to deliver.

Fasting and Prayer: Strengthening Your Spiritual Muscles

Jesus emphasized the power of fasting combined with prayer in Matthew 17:21 when His disciples could not cast out a demon. He explained that "this kind does not go out except by prayer and fasting." Fasting is a spiritual discipline that enhances your sensitivity to God's voice, breaks the chains of spiritual bondage, and brings about divine intervention.

As you embark on this journey, consider setting aside regular times for fasting. Seek the Lord on how long and how often you should fast. It could be a day each week or a longer period as the Holy Spirit leads. During your fast, pray specifically for your son's deliverance, asking God to reveal the root causes of any spiritual oppression he faces. Pray for wisdom, discernment, and divine strategies to confront and dismantle these strongholds.

Fasting aligns your heart with God's heart, purifies your intentions, and amplifies your spiritual authority. It is a way of saying, "God, I depend on You alone. I seek Your face above all else." Through fasting, you deny your flesh and strengthen your spirit, making you more attuned to the spiritual realities around you.

Engaging in Spiritual Warfare: Understanding Your Authority

The battle for your son's deliverance requires an understanding of the authority you possess in Christ. Ephesians 6:12 reminds us that "we do not wrestle against flesh and blood, but against principalities, against powers, against the rulers of the darkness of this world, against spiritual wickedness in high places." This is a spiritual battle, and you must recognize that your authority comes from Jesus Christ, who has already defeated the enemy.

Luke 10:19 declares, "Behold, I give unto you power to tread on serpents and scorpions, and over all the power of the enemy: and nothing shall by any means hurt you." You have been given power and authority to trample over every scheme of the enemy. Exercise this authority boldly in prayer, declaring God's Word over your son. Speak life where there is death, hope where there is despair, and freedom where there is bondage.

Take practical steps to engage in spiritual warfare:
- Anoint your son's room with oil, symbolizing the presence and protection of the Holy Spirit.
- Lay hands on your son and pray for his deliverance, asking God to break every chain that holds him captive.
- Rebuke any spirit of rebellion, addiction, or fear in Jesus' name. Declare that your son belongs to God and that no weapon formed against him shall prosper.

Surrounding Yourself with a Prayer Support Network

No battle should be fought alone. Surround yourself with a network of prayer warriors who can stand with you in agreement for your son's deliverance. Ecclesiastes 4:12 says, "Though one may be overpowered, two can defend themselves. A cord of three strands is not quickly broken." This scripture underscores the power of unity in prayer.

Find trusted friends, family members, or church leaders who are seasoned in prayer and spiritual warfare. Share your concerns with them and ask for their intercession. Be mindful to choose those who will commit to confidentiality, fervency, and faithfulness in prayer. Consider organizing a prayer group or chain where people take turns praying for your son daily.

When you feel weary, their prayers will lift you up. When doubt creeps in, their faith will strengthen yours. Together, you will form a spiritual army, advancing against the enemy's territory and claiming victory in Jesus' name.

Walking in Faith, Not by Sight

Preparing spiritually for your son's deliverance is about aligning yourself with God's will, standing firm on His promises, and believing that He is more than able to deliver and restore. It is about embracing your role as a warrior in God's army, fully equipped and ready for battle. Remember, the journey will have its challenges, but with God on your side, victory is assured. As you prepare, rest in the assurance that the God who called you to this battle is faithful to see you through. Stand firm, pray boldly, and watch as God moves mightily in your son's life.

Deliverance Prayers

1. Heavenly Father, I come before you in the mighty name of Jesus, taking authority over every spiritual attack against my son. I declare that no weapon formed against him shall prosper, and every tongue that rises against him in judgment, I condemn in Jesus' name. Lord, reveal to me the hidden battles he faces and grant me the discernment to pray effectively for his freedom.

2. Lord Jesus, I recognize the enemy's plans to steal, kill, and destroy my son's destiny. Today, I take a stand in the authority you have given me, and I break every chain of bondage and every spiritual attack coming against him. I declare that my son belongs to you, and the gates of hell shall not prevail against him.

3. Father, in Jesus' name, I bind and cast out every spirit of confusion, depression, and fear trying to operate in my son's life. I speak clarity of mind, peace, and divine order into his life right now. Let your Holy Spirit fill him with strength, courage, and a sound mind.

4. I declare in Jesus' name that my son is covered by the blood of Jesus. I break every generational curse, spoken word, and evil assignment against

him. Lord, protect him from every scheme of the enemy, and let your light expose every hidden work of darkness.

5. Lord, I ask that you surround my son with your angels, keeping him safe from all harm. In the name of Jesus, I come against every spirit of darkness that seeks to invade his mind, his thoughts, and his heart. I speak life, hope, and divine protection over him.

6. Heavenly Father, I ask you to open my eyes to any signs of spiritual oppression that may be affecting my son. In Jesus' name, I rebuke any spirit of heaviness, anxiety, or despair that seeks to take hold of him. I declare freedom and peace over his mind and spirit.

7. Lord, in Jesus' name, I break the chains of addiction, rebellion, and defiance that have tried to take root in my son's life. I command every oppressive force to flee, and I plead the blood of Jesus over his thoughts, emotions, and actions.

8. Father, I come against every spirit of anger, frustration, and aggression in my son's life. In the name of Jesus, I bind these spirits and cast them out. Fill my son with your love, patience, and kindness. Let him experience your peace that surpasses all understanding.

9. In Jesus' name, I command any spirit of fear, doubt, or unbelief to leave my son now. I declare that he has not been given a spirit of fear, but of

power, love, and a sound mind. Lord, help him to walk confidently in his identity as a child of God.

10. Lord Jesus, I take authority over every spiritual stronghold trying to keep my son bound. I break the hold of every lie, every deceit, and every manipulation of the enemy. I speak your truth over him, that he is loved, valued, and chosen by you.

11. Father, in the name of Jesus, I break the power of addiction over my son's life. I command every spirit of addiction, whether to substances, screens, or destructive behaviors, to loose its hold on him. I declare that he is free from all chains and filled with a desire for holiness and purity.

12. In Jesus' name, I come against the spirit of anger that seeks to destroy my son's peace and relationships. I command it to be removed from his life right now. Lord, replace his anger with a spirit of gentleness and self-control. Let your peace reign in his heart.

13. Lord, I take authority over the spirit of anxiety that is trying to dominate my son's mind. I speak your peace into his life, declaring that anxiety has no place in him. Your Word says to cast all our cares upon you, for you care for us. I pray that my son will trust in you with all his heart.

14. Heavenly Father, I stand against the spirit of confusion and mental oppression in my son's life. I declare clarity, purpose, and divine wisdom

to flow over him. In Jesus' name, I bind every mental stronghold and replace it with your truth.

15. Jesus, I pray that every stronghold of sin and addiction in my son's life is broken right now. I declare that he is no longer a slave to sin but a child of the Most High God, redeemed by the blood of the Lamb and empowered by your Spirit to live in freedom.

16. Lord, I acknowledge my role as a spiritual guardian over my son. In Jesus' name, I pray for wisdom, strength, and courage to stand in the gap for him. I ask for a heightened discernment to recognize any spiritual attacks and the authority to break them in your name.

17. Heavenly Father, I commit myself to pray daily for my son's spiritual well-being. I ask you to equip me with the words, the insights, and the strategies needed to cover him in prayer effectively. In Jesus' name, I declare that no evil shall befall him while I stand in the gap.

18. Father, in Jesus' name, help me to see my son as you see him—precious, valuable, and loved. I take authority over any spirit of discouragement or failure that tries to take root in his life. I will speak life, faith, and encouragement over him every day.

19. In the mighty name of Jesus, I stand as a gatekeeper over my home and family. I declare that no evil spirit, no dark influence, and no wicked

scheme will cross the threshold of my home. Lord, fill our home with your presence and peace.

20. Jesus, I take my role seriously as a spiritual watchman over my son. In your name, I ask for the boldness to confront any evil influence, the wisdom to discern his needs, and the strength to pray fervently for his deliverance and growth in you.

21. Heavenly Father, I prepare myself spiritually for the journey ahead by putting on the full armor of God. In Jesus' name, I take up the shield of faith, the sword of the Spirit, and the helmet of salvation. I declare that I am ready to battle in prayer for my son's deliverance.

22. Lord, in Jesus' name, I ask for a fresh outpouring of your Holy Spirit upon me. Fill me with your power, wisdom, and guidance as I prepare to intercede for my son. Help me to pray with authority, boldness, and unwavering faith.

23. Father, as I embark on this journey of prayer and deliverance, I pray for protection against any counterattacks of the enemy. In Jesus' name, I declare that you are my shield and fortress. No harm will come near me or my family as we stand firm in your truth.

24. In Jesus' name, I declare that I will not grow weary or faint-hearted in this spiritual battle. Lord, give me the endurance to persist in prayer, the

strength to overcome obstacles, and the courage to stand firm in faith until my son is fully delivered.

25. Lord Jesus, I dedicate this journey of deliverance to you. I pray for your wisdom, guidance, and protection as I navigate the spiritual realms on behalf of my son. In Jesus' name, I declare victory over every scheme of the enemy and a future filled with hope and purpose for my son.

Chapter 2

Praying for Protection:
Covering Your Son with the Blood of Jesus

The Power of the Blood:
Biblical Foundation and Understanding

In the journey of deliverance and spiritual warfare, one of the most potent weapons God has given us is the blood of Jesus Christ. When it comes to protecting our teenage sons from the enemy's attacks, few things are as powerful as understanding and applying the blood of Jesus in prayer.

Understanding the Significance of the Blood of Jesus

The blood of Jesus is not just a symbolic element of Christianity; it is the very essence of our redemption and protection. From the earliest passages of the Bible, blood is presented as a necessary means of atonement and reconciliation with God. In the Old Testament, the sacrificial system, particularly in the book of Leviticus, established the principle that "without the shedding of blood, there is no forgiveness" (Hebrews 9:22). However, these sacrifices were only temporary, pointing to a future, ultimate sacrifice — the blood of Jesus.

When Jesus Christ, the spotless Lamb of God, died on the cross, His blood was shed for the redemption of all mankind. This was not just any blood; it was divine, sinless, and eternal. It carried the weight of God's righteousness, holiness, and love. The blood of Jesus has the power to cleanse, protect, redeem, and deliver. Revelation 12:11 declares, "And they overcame him by the blood of the Lamb and by the word of their testimony." This verse highlights the dual power of the blood of Jesus and our declarations in overcoming the enemy. When you pray for your teenage son, you are invoking the same overcoming power.

Why the Blood? A Deeper Spiritual Reality

But why focus on the blood? In the spiritual realm, the blood of Jesus represents the ultimate victory over sin, death, and the devil. It is a legal currency in the courts of heaven, testifying that every accusation the enemy brings against us has been nullified. The blood speaks of forgiveness, but it also speaks of protection. In Exodus 12, during the first Passover, God instructed the Israelites to apply the blood of a lamb to the doorposts of their homes so that the angel of death would pass over them. This was a foreshadowing of the greater protection provided by the blood of Jesus.

For your teenage son, this means that when you pray and apply the blood of Jesus over his life, you are marking him with divine protection. The enemy sees this mark and knows that he has no legal right to attack, harass, or oppress your son. The blood of Jesus becomes a barrier, a shield, and a fortress around him.

Strategic Prayers: How to Apply the Blood of Jesus Over Your Son

To cover your son with the blood of Jesus, your prayers need to be specific, authoritative, and filled with faith. Here are steps to strategically pray and apply the blood of Jesus over your teenage son:

- Begin with Thanksgiving and Worship: Before you declare anything, start by acknowledging God's sovereignty and thanking Him for the power of the blood. Praise Him for the provision of protection and salvation. This sets the atmosphere for your prayer and aligns your heart with God's will.

- Confess Any Known Sin: Confession is a crucial step. Sin, whether known or unknown, can create gaps in the spiritual hedge of protection around your son. Stand in the gap as a parent and confess any sins on behalf of your son and your family, asking for God's forgiveness. Claim 1 John 1:9, which promises, "If we confess our sins, He is faithful and just to forgive us our sins and to cleanse us from all unrighteousness."

- Declare the Power of the Blood: Now, boldly declare the power of the blood of Jesus over your son. Speak it out loud. Say, "I apply the blood of Jesus over [your son's name]. I declare that he is protected, redeemed, and covered by the blood of the Lamb. No weapon formed against him shall prosper (Isaiah 54:17)." Use your words to build a spiritual fortress around him.

- Pray for Specific Areas of His Life: Don't be vague; cover specific areas of your son's life in prayer. Pray over his mind, emotions, body, relationships, and decisions. Say, "I cover [your son's name]'s mind with the blood of Jesus. I declare that every thought is captive to the obedience of Christ (2 Corinthians 10:5). I cover his emotions with the blood of Jesus, that he may experience peace, joy, and stability."

- Rebuke the Enemy in the Name of Jesus: With the authority you have in Christ, command any evil presence or influence to leave your son alone. Say, "In the name of Jesus, I rebuke every spirit of fear, confusion, rebellion, addiction, and oppression. I command you to flee from [your son's name], for he is covered by the blood of Jesus."

Living Under the Blood: Cultivating a Daily Habit of Prayer

Applying the blood of Jesus over your son is not a one-time event; it is a daily habit. Just as the Israelites had to renew their commitment to God daily, we, too, must continually cover our children in prayer. Make it a point to pray for your son each day, not just when you see trouble, but even when everything seems calm. This proactive stance keeps the enemy at bay and reinforces the spiritual hedge around him.

Encourage your son to understand the power of the blood of Jesus and to use it in his own prayers. Teach him to declare, "I am covered by the blood of Jesus. No evil shall befall me, and no plague shall come near my dwelling (Psalm 91:10)." When your son understands his authority in Christ and the significance of the blood, he becomes an active participant in his spiritual protection.

Faith in Action: Trusting in God's Unfailing Protection

Finally, remember that your prayers, empowered by faith and the Word of God, are mighty and effective. Hebrews 4:16 encourages us to "come boldly to the throne of grace, that we may obtain mercy and find grace to help in time of need." Trust that God hears your prayers and that the blood of Jesus is at work, shielding, guarding, and protecting your son.

Praying the blood of Jesus over your teenage son is not just a ritual; it is an act of spiritual warfare, a declaration of God's sovereignty, and a proclamation of victory over every scheme of the enemy. As you continue to cover your son with the blood of Jesus, you align yourself with God's divine protection plan and witness His power manifest in your son's life in extraordinary ways.

Prayers for Spiritual Covering and Divine Protection

The Shield of Divine Protection

In the battle for your son's spiritual health and destiny, the greatest weapon in your arsenal is prayer—prayers that call upon the blood of Jesus as a protective shield. As parents, we are not merely caregivers; we are spiritual warriors called to stand in the gap for our children, especially in their teenage years, when they face immense pressures and temptations. Praying for spiritual covering and divine protection over your son is an act of faith and a declaration of God's sovereignty over his life.

Understanding the Power of the Blood of Jesus

Before delving into specific prayers, it is essential to understand why the blood of Jesus is so powerful. In Christian doctrine, the blood of Jesus Christ is not just a historical event but an ongoing spiritual reality. It represents the ultimate sacrifice that Jesus made on the cross for the remission of sins and the defeat of every power of darkness (Hebrews 9:22). The blood of Jesus is alive and active; it is the "better word" that speaks on behalf of believers (Hebrews 12:24). When we plead the blood of Jesus over our children, we are invoking all the authority and victory that Jesus achieved through His death and resurrection.

Praying for Divine Protection: Setting the Spiritual Atmosphere

To pray effectively for your son's protection, you must first set the spiritual atmosphere in your home. Begin with worship, allowing your heart to focus on God's greatness and His promises. Sing songs that exalt the name of Jesus and declare His lordship over your household. Worship invites the presence of God, and where God is present, no enemy can stand. As you worship, visualize the blood of Jesus covering your son like a divine cloak—a barrier that no evil can penetrate.

Prayer Point 1: Pleading the Blood of Jesus Over Your Son's Mind

The mind is the battlefield where many spiritual battles are fought and lost. Teenagers, especially, are bombarded with messages from the world, social media, and even their peers that can plant seeds of doubt, fear, rebellion, or immorality. As you pray, declare that your son's mind is protected by the blood of Jesus. Speak scriptures like Philippians 4:7, which promises that "the peace of God, which surpasses all understanding, will guard your hearts and minds in Christ Jesus." Proclaim that every negative thought is taken captive to obey Christ (2 Corinthians 10:5).

Sample Prayer:
"Father, in the name of Jesus, I plead the blood of Jesus over [Son's Name]'s mind. I declare that his thoughts are aligned with your Word and that he will not conform to the patterns of this world. Let every lie of the enemy be exposed and destroyed by the power of the blood of Jesus. I proclaim that he has the mind of Christ, filled with wisdom, peace, and divine understanding. Amen."

Prayer Point 2: Covering Your Son's Emotions and Heart

Teenage years are often marked by intense emotions—anger, insecurity, anxiety, and sometimes despair. These emotions can become doorways through which the enemy seeks to gain a foothold. Pray for the blood of Jesus to cover your son's heart, protecting him from emotional wounds that could lead to bitterness, unforgiveness, or rebellion.

Sample Prayer:
"Lord Jesus, I plead your blood over [Son's Name]'s heart and emotions. May he be rooted and grounded in your love, which casts out all fear. I declare that no weapon formed against his emotional well-being will prosper. Heal any wounds, seen or unseen, and fill his heart with joy and peace. Let your love be the anchor of his soul, and may he always find comfort and strength in you. In Jesus' name, Amen."

Prayer Point 3: Shielding Against Spiritual Attacks and Temptations

Teenagers face many spiritual attacks—from peer pressure to succumb to addictions, to the lure of sexual immorality, to the influence of false doctrines. Pray specifically against these temptations, invoking the blood of Jesus to shield your son from every snare the enemy has set for him.

Sample Prayer:
"Father, I come against every temptation and spiritual attack that the enemy has planned against [Son's Name]. I cover him with the blood of Jesus, declaring that he will stand firm in the day of trial. I rebuke every spirit of addiction, immorality, rebellion, and confusion. I declare that the

blood of Jesus is a wall of fire around him, a shield that deflects every fiery dart of the enemy. In Jesus' mighty name, I pray. Amen."

Prayer Point 4: Declaring Physical Protection and Safety

Beyond spiritual and emotional protection, we must also pray for our children's physical safety. Teenagers are often involved in activities that can put them at risk, whether through travel, sports, or everyday encounters. Ask for the blood of Jesus to protect your son from accidents, injuries, and any physical harm.

Sample Prayer:
"Lord, I plead the blood of Jesus over [Son's Name]'s physical body. I declare that no harm shall befall him, no plague shall come near his dwelling. I proclaim Psalm 91 over him—that you will command your angels concerning him to guard him in all his ways. I speak life, health, and divine protection over every step he takes. In Jesus' name, Amen."

Prayer Point 5: Covering His Future and Destiny with the Blood of Jesus

The teenage years are critical for shaping your son's future. Pray for God's divine purpose and destiny to be fulfilled in his life. Ask for the blood of Jesus to cover every decision, every step, and every relationship he engages in.

Sample Prayer:

"Father, I lift up [Son's Name] to you, pleading the blood of Jesus over his future and destiny. I declare that no plan of the enemy will prosper against him. He is marked for your kingdom, set apart for your purpose. Guide him, Lord, in the path of righteousness for your name's sake. May he walk in the fullness of his calling, untainted by the world, and always sensitive to your leading. In the mighty name of Jesus, I pray. Amen."

Living in the Reality of Divine Protection

Praying for spiritual covering and divine protection over your son is not a one-time act but a continuous, daily commitment. It is living in the reality of God's promises, recognizing that the blood of Jesus is powerful and effective today as it was at Calvary. As you pray, believe that God hears your petitions and is faithful to protect, guide, and bless your son. Trust that His blood will never lose its power and that your son is secure in His loving care. Let your prayers become a daily mantle of divine protection that your son carries with him wherever he goes, knowing that no weapon formed against him shall prosper, and every tongue that rises against him in judgment will be condemned (Isaiah 54:17).

Declaring Psalm 91 Over Your Son's Life

Psalm 91 is a powerful Scripture that provides divine assurance of God's protection and deliverance in times of trouble. When it comes to our teenage sons, navigating the challenging world of adolescence, this psalm becomes a fortress of safety, a shield against the unseen battles they face daily. As parents, it is our spiritual responsibility to stand in the gap and declare God's promises over our children.

Understanding the Power of Psalm 91

Psalm 91 is often referred to as the "Psalm of Protection." It is a declaration of God's sovereignty, power, and promise to safeguard His people from harm. The psalm begins with a powerful statement: "He who dwells in the secret place of the Most High shall abide under the shadow of the Almighty" (Psalm 91:1, NKJV). This verse sets the tone for the entire psalm, emphasizing the need for intimate communion with God—a place where God's presence becomes a shield around us.

For your teenage son, declaring Psalm 91 is more than just reciting words; it is a spiritual act of warfare. It is an intentional proclamation of God's promises, affirming your son's place in the shadow of the Almighty, a position of divine safety where the enemy's darts cannot penetrate. Each verse of Psalm 91 holds a promise, a shield of faith that covers your son from the crown of his head to the soles of his feet.

How to Declare Psalm 91 Over Your Son

1. Personalize the Verses: Speak Them with Authority

Begin by personalizing the verses of Psalm 91 for your son. Replace the pronouns in the scripture with your son's name. For example, declare, "Because [Your Son's Name] dwells in the secret place of the Most High, he shall abide under the shadow of the Almighty. [Your Son's Name] will say of the Lord, 'He is my refuge and my fortress; my God, in Him I will trust.'" Speak these words with authority, understanding that as a parent, God has entrusted you with spiritual authority over your son. When you declare these words, you are not just reading Scripture; you are releasing God's divine protection over his life.

2. Engage in Strategic Prayer: Claim the Promises

Psalm 91 contains several promises of protection—deliverance from the snare of the fowler, protection from deadly pestilence, immunity from terror by night and arrows by day, and divine guardianship by His angels. Claim these promises specifically in prayer. For instance, declare that "No weapon formed against [Your Son's Name] shall prosper," and that "a thousand may fall at his side, and ten thousand at his right hand, but it shall not come near him" (Psalm 91:7, NKJV). Pray that every scheme, plot, or plan of the enemy be dismantled by the power of God's Word.

3. Visualize the Protection: See the Angels Surrounding Your Son

Engage your spiritual imagination. As you declare Psalm 91, visualize the angelic hosts surrounding your son. The Bible says, "For He shall give His angels charge over you, to keep you in all your ways" (Psalm 91:11,

NKJV). Imagine these angels as mighty warriors, standing guard over your son wherever he goes—whether at school, with friends, or even in the privacy of his room. This visualization isn't just an exercise in imagination; it's an act of faith. Remember, the spiritual realm responds to faith, and your words, spoken in alignment with God's Word, activate this divine protection.

4. Incorporate Worship: Seal the Declaration with Praise

Once you have declared Psalm 91, seal it with worship and praise. Thank God in advance for His protection over your son. Worship acknowledges that the battle belongs to the Lord and that He is already at work. Remember the story of King Jehoshaphat in 2 Chronicles 20:21-22, where God instructed the Israelites to send worshipers ahead of the army. As they began to sing and praise, the Lord set ambushes against their enemies. In the same way, let your worship be a weapon that sets spiritual ambushes against any force seeking to harm your son.

Why Psalm 91 is Particularly Relevant for Teenagers Today

Teenagers today face unique spiritual challenges. The constant bombardment of secular media, peer pressure, and a culture often hostile to faith can make them susceptible to fear, anxiety, depression, and spiritual confusion. Declaring Psalm 91 over your son is an act of reclaiming his identity in Christ, a reminder that he is not defined by the world but by the promises of God.

In addition, this Psalm addresses specific fears that many teenagers face—fear of the unknown ("the terror by night"), fear of violence ("the arrow that flies by day"), fear of illness ("the pestilence that walks in darkness"), and fear of sudden disaster ("the destruction that lays waste at noonday"). By declaring this psalm, you are prophetically speaking peace, courage, and divine immunity into your son's life.

Overcoming Opposition: The Boldness of a Parent's Faith

Understand that as you declare Psalm 91 over your son, you are engaging in spiritual warfare. Expect resistance from the enemy, but do not be discouraged. Remember, your authority as a parent is recognized in the spiritual realm. The enemy knows this, and he trembles at the sound of a parent who prays with faith. The Bible assures us that the "effective, fervent prayer of a righteous man avails much" (James 5:16, NKJV). Stand firm, knowing that you are not fighting this battle alone—God is with you, and His Word is your weapon.

Standing in the Gap with Psalm 91

Declaring Psalm 91 over your son is an act of spiritual protection that places him under God's divine covering. It is a reminder that, despite the challenges he may face, he is secure under the shadow of the Almighty. Continue to declare this powerful psalm daily, trusting that God's promises are true and that His protection is unwavering. Know that your prayers are a lifeline, a spiritual shield that no enemy can penetrate. Through your faith and persistent prayer, God will move mightily on behalf of your son, safeguarding his mind, body, and spirit from all harm.

Stand boldly, declare Psalm 91 with confidence, and watch as God's protective hand moves over your son's life, guiding him safely through the trials and tribulations of his teenage years into the destiny God has ordained for him.

Breaking Generational Curses and Negative Patterns

Generational curses are a spiritual reality that often affects the lives of individuals, including our teenage sons. These curses, which may manifest as repetitive patterns of sin, negative behavior, or destructive habits passed down through family lines, can bind a person to a cycle of spiritual oppression. However, as believers, we have the authority through Christ to break these generational curses and patterns, reclaiming our family's spiritual freedom.

Understanding Generational Curses

Generational curses are mentioned throughout the Bible, illustrating that sins and iniquities can affect future generations. For example, in Exodus 34:7, God speaks of visiting "the iniquity of the fathers upon the children and the children's children to the third and the fourth generation." This passage reveals that patterns of sin, rebellion, and disobedience can have lasting effects on our descendants. These curses are not merely random misfortunes but spiritual consequences of disobedience to God's commandments.

However, in the new covenant through Jesus Christ, we are not bound by these curses. Galatians 3:13 tells us, "Christ has redeemed us from the curse of the law, having become a curse for us." This verse affirms that through Jesus' sacrifice, we have been set free from every form of curse, including those that may have plagued our families for generations.

Identifying Generational Curses in Your Son's Life

Before we can effectively pray against generational curses, it is crucial to recognize their presence in your son's life. Generational curses may manifest in various forms such as:

- Addictions (alcohol, drugs, pornography, gambling)
- Chronic illnesses (depression, anxiety, hereditary diseases)
- Patterns of failure (financial struggles, relationship breakdowns)
- Negative behavioral traits (anger, rebellion, lying, pride)
- Spiritual stagnation (lack of interest in spiritual growth, rejection of faith)

Take time to prayerfully examine the history of your family, discerning patterns or repeated issues that seem to plague multiple generations. This reflection can be guided by the Holy Spirit, who reveals hidden truths and areas where bondage needs to be broken.

Prayer Strategy for Breaking Generational Curses

To break generational curses, we must approach prayer boldly, wielding the spiritual authority given to us through Christ. Here is a step-by-step strategy to help you pray effectively for your teenage son:

- Confession and Repentance: Begin by confessing any known sins that may have contributed to the curse. This is not only a personal confession but also a stand-in intercessory confession for your ancestors who may have sinned. As Nehemiah confessed the sins of his people (Nehemiah 1:6-7), so should we stand in the gap and repent for our family line. Pray, "Lord, I confess and repent of any sins in my family line that have opened doors to generational curses. I ask for Your forgiveness and cleansing through the blood of Jesus."

- Renunciation of Agreements: Declare out loud that you break any agreement, knowingly or unknowingly, that your family or your son has made with the enemy. Renunciation is a powerful spiritual act that nullifies any covenants or pacts made by previous generations. Pray, "In the name of Jesus, I renounce and break every agreement made with the forces of darkness by myself, my ancestors, or my son. I sever every tie and cancel every assignment of the enemy against my family."

- Pleading the Blood of Jesus: The blood of Jesus is our ultimate weapon in spiritual warfare. Revelation 12:11 states, "And they overcame him by the blood of the Lamb and by the word of their testimony." Plead the blood of Jesus over your son, declaring that every curse, bondage, and negative pattern is broken by the power of the blood. Pray, "I plead the blood of Jesus over my son. The blood that speaks a better word than the blood of Abel (Hebrews 12:24) breaks every generational curse, every bondage, and every demonic stronghold in his life."

- Declaring Freedom and Blessing: Declare freedom over your son, speaking God's promises and blessings into his life. This step is vital as it replaces the curses with God's truth. Pray, "I declare in the name of Jesus that my son is free from every generational curse. I proclaim that he is blessed with the blessings of Abraham, that he walks in righteousness, favor, and divine health, and that no weapon formed against him shall prosper (Isaiah 54:17)."

- Thanksgiving and Faith Declaration: End your prayer with thanksgiving, expressing faith in God's deliverance. Pray, "Father, I thank You for breaking every curse and setting my son free. I believe in Your promises, and I know that You are faithful to complete the good work You have begun in him (Philippians 1:6). I declare that my son will walk in the fullness of his destiny in Christ."

Going Beyond Prayer: Building a Curse-Free Legacy

Breaking generational curses is not just a one-time event; it is an ongoing spiritual discipline. Encourage your son to develop his relationship with God, equipping him with the knowledge of his identity in Christ. Teach him the power of confession, repentance, and speaking God's Word over his life.

Additionally, consider incorporating these practices into your family life:
- Regular Family Prayer: Establish a routine of praying together as a family, breaking curses, and declaring blessings over each other.
- Daily Scripture Reading: Engage in daily Bible study and meditation on God's Word, which renews the mind and dismantles lies of the enemy.
- Fasting: Dedicate periods of fasting for greater spiritual insight and breakthrough.
- Accountability and Support: Create a supportive environment where open communication about spiritual matters is encouraged, and your son feels empowered to share his struggles and victories.

By engaging in these spiritual practices, you create an atmosphere where the presence of God dwells, and where generational curses have no foothold. Remember, in Christ, you are more than conquerors (Romans 8:37), and every curse is broken under the mighty name of Jesus. Stand firm in faith, believing that your son is set free and that he will walk in his God-given destiny.

Sealing Your Son's Future with God's Promises

When praying for the deliverance and spiritual protection of your teenage son, it is crucial to understand the power of God's promises as both a shield and a source of hope. God's promises are not merely words written on paper; they are alive, powerful, and eternal, capable of transforming your son's life and securing his future in Christ.

Understanding God's Promises: A Foundation of Faith

The Bible is filled with promises from God that cover every aspect of human life—protection, provision, healing, guidance, and deliverance. These promises serve as an anchor for our faith, especially during tumultuous times. For your son, whose life is at a critical crossroads, God's promises are like signposts that guide him toward God's perfect will and keep him on the path of righteousness.

To begin, it's essential to understand that God's promises are certain. Numbers 23:19 (NIV) declares, "God is not human, that he should lie, not a human being, that he should change his mind. Does he speak and then not act? Does he promise and not fulfill?" This verse underlines the absolute reliability of God's Word. When we pray over our children, we are not making mere wishes; we are aligning ourselves with the infallible, unchanging will of God.

Claiming God's Promises: A Spiritual Inheritance

Every believer has the right to claim God's promises as their spiritual inheritance. For your son, these promises are a treasure trove of spiritual wealth that he can access at any time. But how do we go from knowing the promises to actively claiming them for our children?

First, it involves recognizing that these promises are secured in Christ. 2 Corinthians 1:20 (NIV) reminds us, "For no matter how many promises God has made, they are 'Yes' in Christ. And so through him, the 'Amen' is spoken by us to the glory of God." This verse indicates that every promise God made is fulfilled through Jesus. Therefore, when praying for your son, invoke the name of Jesus, who is the guarantor of every divine promise.

For instance, pray Scriptures over your son. Declare Psalm 138:8 (NIV): "The Lord will fulfill his purpose for [your son]; your steadfast love, O Lord, endures forever." By doing this, you are reminding God of His Word and standing on His promise that He will complete what He started in your son's life.

Declaring God's Promises: Speaking Life and Truth Over Your Son

The power of life and death is in the tongue (Proverbs 18:21). Declaring God's promises over your son is not a passive act; it is a spiritual weapon that cuts through the lies of the enemy. The world, social media, peer pressure, and even internal fears can bombard your son with negative messages about who he is and who he can become. But you have the authority, as a parent and a believer, to declare God's truth over him.

Start by speaking promises that counter the lies he might be believing. If he struggles with self-worth or identity, declare Jeremiah 29:11 (NIV): "For I know the plans I have for you," declares the Lord, "plans to prosper you and not to harm you, plans to give you hope and a future." Let this promise saturate his heart and mind, dismantling any negative self-image the enemy has planted.

Be bold in your declarations. Do not merely whisper these promises in a corner; proclaim them with authority, knowing that you are backed by Heaven. Jesus said in Matthew 18:18 (NIV), "Truly I tell you, whatever you bind on earth will be bound in heaven, and whatever you loose on earth will be loosed in heaven." Use this spiritual authority to bind every plan of the enemy against your son and loose God's promises into his life.

Practical Steps: Engraving God's Promises into Your Son's Heart

To seal your son's future with God's promises, it's essential to make these promises a regular part of his life. Here are some practical steps to help you do this:

- Create a Promise Journal: Encourage your son to keep a journal specifically for God's promises. Every day or week, write down a promise from Scripture and reflect on how it applies to his life. This simple practice will help him internalize God's Word and make it personal.

- Daily Declarations Together: Set aside time each day to declare God's promises together. Speak them out loud, pray them, and discuss their meaning. Make this a habit, a part of your daily routine. This not only strengthens his faith but also yours as a parent.

- Memorization and Meditation: Challenge your son to memorize key promises from Scripture. Teach him to meditate on these promises, allowing them to saturate his thoughts. When temptations or challenges arise, these promises will become his immediate defense, reminding him of God's truth.

- Visual Reminders: Place visual reminders of God's promises around your home. Print Scriptures and hang them in his room, on the fridge, or in other common areas. Let your environment reflect the truth of God's Word and remind him of God's faithfulness.

- Incorporate Promises in Daily Prayer: When you pray for your son, always incorporate specific promises from the Bible. Remind God of His Word and affirm your faith in His power to fulfill those promises. Encourage your son to do the same in his prayers.

The Power of Persistence: Never Ceasing in Faith

Remember, sealing your son's future with God's prom... time event but a continuous process. It involves persistent, unwavering faith, and a steadfast commitment to God's Word. Even when circumstances seem contrary, keep declaring, keep believing, and keep trusting that God is faithful to fulfill every promise concerning your son.

Isaiah 55:11 (NIV) assures us, "So is my word that goes out from my mouth: It will not return to me empty, but will accomplish what I desire and achieve the purpose for which I sent it." When you pray and declare God's promises over your son, you are releasing words that are alive and active, words that have the power to change his destiny and secure his future in God's hands.

Let this be your anchor in times of doubt or difficulty. Continue to speak life, truth, and victory over your son, trusting that God's promises will indeed come to pass, sealing his future in the love, grace, and protection of the Almighty.

Deliverance Prayers

1. Heavenly Father, I come before you, acknowledging the power in the blood of Jesus Christ. I plead the blood of Jesus over my son's life, believing that it washes away all sin, breaks every chain, and sets him free from every bondage. In Jesus' name, I declare that the blood speaks a better word over his life than any curse, accusation, or lie of the enemy.

2. Lord Jesus, I thank you for your sacrificial death and the blood you shed for the redemption of all. I take authority in your name and decree that the power of your blood covers my son, protecting him from every attack of the enemy, every spirit of darkness, and every evil plan against his destiny.

3. Father, I claim the blood of Jesus over my son's mind, body, and spirit. I rebuke every spirit of fear, doubt, and confusion that tries to attack him, and I declare that the blood of Jesus stands against them. No weapon formed against him shall prosper because of the blood that was shed for his victory.

4. Lord, I cover my son in the blood of Jesus from the crown of his head to the soles of his feet. I declare that he is marked by the blood and that every evil force, spirit of affliction, or curse must pass over him because of the blood of the Lamb.

5. In the name of Jesus, I declare that the blood of Christ has redeemed my son from every curse of the law, every generational curse, and every spirit of bondage. I stand on the power of the blood and decree that my son is free, whole, and delivered in Jesus' name.

6. Almighty God, I come before you, asking for divine protection over my son. Surround him with your heavenly host, and may your presence go before him, behind him, and beside him in all his ways. Keep him safe from harm, accidents, and every hidden trap of the enemy.

7. Father, I pray for your spiritual covering over my son. I ask that you be his refuge and fortress, his ever-present help in times of trouble. Hide him under the shadow of your wings, where no evil can touch him.

8. Lord Jesus, I speak divine protection over my son's heart, mind, and spirit. Guard him against any negative influences, harmful relationships, and ungodly counsel. Cover him with your peace that surpasses all understanding, that he may stand firm in his faith.

9. Father, I declare that no weapon formed against my son shall prosper. Every tongue that rises against him in judgment, I condemn in the name of Jesus. I plead the blood of Jesus over him, creating a divine barrier that the enemy cannot penetrate.

10. Lord, I ask that you assign your angels to encamp around my son wherever he goes. Keep him safe from all spiritual and physical harm, and protect him from any scheme of the enemy designed to derail his destiny.

11. Father, I declare Psalm 91 over my son's life: that he will dwell in the secret place of the Most High and abide under the shadow of the Almighty. I proclaim that you are his refuge and fortress, and in you, he will trust.

12. Lord, I decree that my son will not fear the terror by night, nor the arrow that flies by day. A thousand may fall at his side, and ten thousand

at his right hand, but it will not come near him because you are his shield and defender.

13. Father, I pray that you will deliver my son from every snare of the fowler and from the perilous pestilence. Cover him with your feathers, and let him find refuge under your wings. Let your faithfulness be his shield and rampart.

14. I declare that my son will not fear any evil, for you, Lord, are with him. Your angels will bear him up in their hands, lest he dash his foot against a stone. I proclaim that he is covered, shielded, and protected by your mighty hand.

15. Lord, I decree that no evil shall befall my son, nor shall any plague come near his dwelling. Because he has set his love upon you, you will deliver him, honor him, and satisfy him with long life, and show him your salvation.

16. In the name of Jesus, I break every generational curse that has been passed down through my family line. I sever every ungodly soul tie, every spirit of infirmity, addiction, or bondage that seeks to attach itself to my son. I declare that he is free from every negative pattern in Jesus' name.

17. Father, I stand in the gap for my son and renounce every curse spoken against him, whether knowingly or unknowingly. I speak life, blessings,

and favor over him, and I command every curse to be nullified by the power of the blood of Jesus.

18. Lord, I pray that you break every chain of addiction, depression, and anger that may have been inherited through my family line. I declare that my son will walk in freedom, joy, and peace, untouched by the iniquities of past generations.

19. Father, I ask that you expose and uproot every hidden generational stronghold in our family that seeks to ensnare my son. In the name of Jesus, I cancel every negative pattern, every cycle of failure, and every spirit of poverty or lack.

20. I decree that my son is a new creation in Christ Jesus. Every generational curse, every spoken word of failure, and every spirit of bondage has no power over him. He is covered by the blood of Jesus, and his future is secure in God's hands.

21. Heavenly Father, I speak your promises over my son's life, declaring that he is the head and not the tail, above and not beneath. I seal his future with your plans for prosperity, hope, and a bright future, according to Jeremiah 29:11.

22. Lord, I declare that every promise in your Word will come to pass in my son's life. I speak success, favor, and divine opportunities over him, believing that you will guide his steps and establish his path.

23. Father, I thank you that no matter what the enemy tries, my son's future is secure in your hands. I declare that he will fulfill every purpose and plan you have for him, and nothing will hinder him from reaching his divine destiny.

24. Lord, I ask that you cover my son's future with your grace and mercy. May your promises of protection, provision, and peace be his portion all the days of his life, and may he walk in the fullness of your love.

25. In Jesus' name, I seal my son's future with the promise of your Word. I declare that he will be a mighty warrior for your kingdom, a light in the darkness, and a testament of your saving grace. No weapon formed against him shall prosper, and every promise you have spoken over him will be fulfilled.

Chapter 3

Breaking the Chains of Addiction and Unhealthy Influences

Praying for Deliverance from Substance Abuse and Dependency

Addiction, whether to substances, behaviors, or toxic relationships, is one of the most significant spiritual battles faced by teenagers today. Substance abuse, in particular, has become a rampant issue, invading the lives of young people and entangling them in a web of bondage that affects their minds, bodies, and souls. As a parent, you may feel helpless watching your son struggle with these chains, but be encouraged: God has given you powerful weapons to fight for his deliverance.

Understanding the Nature of Addiction: A Spiritual Stronghold

Before we can pray effectively, we must understand the nature of addiction from a Christian perspective. Addiction is not merely a physical or psychological issue; it is also a spiritual stronghold. The Bible speaks about sin as something that "easily entangles" (Hebrews 12:1). Addiction is a manifestation of that entanglement—a force that binds the soul and spirit, creating a dependency on something other than God.

Satan, the enemy of our souls, seeks to exploit this dependency, turning it into a stronghold that keeps our children trapped. John 10:10 reminds us that "the thief comes only to steal and kill and destroy," but Jesus came to give life—abundant and overflowing. We must approach the battle against addiction, understanding that we are not fighting flesh and blood but "against the spiritual forces of evil in the heavenly realms" (Ephesians 6:12).

Step 1: Confronting the Spiritual Root of Addiction

The first step in praying for deliverance is to confront the spiritual root of addiction. Addiction often stems from deeper issues such as rejection, abandonment, fear, or trauma. It can also result from generational curses or unresolved spiritual conflicts. Begin by asking the Holy Spirit to reveal the root cause of your son's addiction. Pray for insight, wisdom, and discernment, knowing that "the Spirit searches all things, even the deep things of God" (1 Corinthians 2:10).

Pray like this:
"Father, in the name of Jesus, I ask you to reveal the root of my son's addiction. Expose every hidden pain, every unresolved trauma, and every lie that the enemy has planted in his mind. Bring to light any generational curse or sin that is feeding this stronghold. Lord, give me the wisdom to see the spiritual root, and grant me the authority to confront it in your name."

Step 2: Breaking the Chains with the Word of God

The Word of God is a double-edged sword (Hebrews 4:12), powerful and effective in breaking spiritual chains. As you pray, wield the Word of God boldly. Declare scriptures that speak directly to the power of God over addiction. Use verses like 1 Corinthians 10:13, which says, "No temptation has overtaken you except what is common to mankind. And God is faithful; he will not let you be tempted beyond what you can bear. But when you are tempted, he will also provide a way out so that you can endure it."

Personalize these scriptures in your prayers. For example:
"Lord, I thank you that there is no temptation that my son faces that is beyond your power to overcome. I declare that you are faithful, and you will provide a way of escape for him. In Jesus' name, I break every chain of addiction off his life. I speak freedom over him, for your Word says that whom the Son sets free is free indeed (John 8:36)."

Step 3: Engaging in Spiritual Warfare: Binding and Loosing

Jesus taught us the power of binding and loosing in Matthew 18:18: "Truly I tell you, whatever you bind on earth will be bound in heaven, and whatever you loose on earth will be loosed in heaven." In this context, binding means to restrict or prohibit the enemy's influence, while loosing refers to releasing God's power and blessings.

Begin by binding the spirits that are fueling the addiction. Pray with authority:

"In the name of Jesus, I bind every spirit of addiction, bondage, and dependency operating in my son's life. I command every demonic force behind this addiction to leave in Jesus' name. You have no place here, for my son is covered by the blood of Jesus and belongs to the Kingdom of God."

Next, loose the power of God's Spirit over your son's life:
"Father, I loose the spirit of self-control, purity, and righteousness over my son. I release your love, peace, and joy into his heart. Let your Holy Spirit fill every void that this addiction has tried to fill. I declare that my son will walk in freedom, and your presence will be his constant companion."

Step 4: Fasting for Breakthrough: Amplifying the Power of Prayer

There are times when deliverance requires fasting in addition to prayer. Jesus said, "This kind can come out only by prayer and fasting" (Mark 9:29). Fasting amplifies your prayers, bringing breakthrough in areas where there seems to be resistance. Choose a day or several days to fast for your son's deliverance, seeking God with all your heart.

Pray like this during your fast:
"Lord, as I fast, I humble myself before you. I ask for a breakthrough in my son's life. Let every chain be broken, every wall come down, and every

demonic influence be cast out. I pray that you would renew his mind, transform his heart, and set him free from every form of bondage."

Step 5: Persevering in Faith: Believing Until You See the Victory

Deliverance is often a process, not a one-time event. The enemy may try to re-establish his hold, but you must persevere in faith. Continue to pray daily for your son, anointing his room with oil, laying hands on him, and declaring his freedom. Remind yourself that "the prayer of a righteous person is powerful and effective" (James 5:16).

Do not grow weary or lose heart. Encourage your son to participate in this journey, teaching him how to pray for himself and resist the enemy. Stand firm in the promise of God's Word that "if the Son sets you free, you will be free indeed" (John 8:36).

Remember, God is a God of deliverance. He delights in setting captives free, and He has equipped you to stand in the gap for your son. Through prayer, fasting, and the Word, you are tearing down strongholds and claiming the victory that Christ has already won.

Breaking Free from Social Media and Digital Addictions

In today's digital age, social media and digital technology have become an inescapable part of daily life, especially for teenagers. While these platforms can serve as tools for connection, learning, and creativity, they have also become breeding grounds for addiction, distraction, and spiritual bondage. The rise of social media addiction is not just a psychological or behavioral issue; it is a spiritual battle for the hearts and minds of our youth. As Christian parents, we must recognize this reality and engage in fervent, intentional prayer to break the chains of digital addiction over our teenage sons.

Recognizing the Signs of Digital Bondage

Social media addiction often masquerades as harmless entertainment or a necessary means of communication. However, the fruits of this addiction reveal its true nature: increased anxiety, depression, a sense of worthlessness, comparison, and a distorted self-image. The Bible warns us against such things in passages like 2 Corinthians 10:5, which calls us to take captive every thought to make it obedient to Christ. When our sons are enslaved to their screens, they may experience difficulty focusing on studies, a decline in face-to-face relationships, irritability when separated from their devices, and even a sense of emptiness or restlessness without constant digital stimulation. These are not just psychological symptoms; they are spiritual strongholds that the enemy uses to bind and distract our children from their God-given purpose.

Understanding the Spiritual Nature of Digital Addiction

Digital addiction, at its core, is a counterfeit of the fulfillment that only God can provide. In John 10:10, Jesus thief comes only to steal, kill, and destroy; I have come that life, and have it to the full." Social media often offers a false of connection, belonging, and validation. It presents a virtual reality that disconnects our sons from true communion with God and the real relationships He desires for them. The enemy uses digital addiction to steal their time, kill their potential, and destroy their identity in Christ.

The Bible tells us that our battle is not against flesh and blood but against spiritual forces of evil (Ephesians 6:12). This truth applies to the battle against digital addiction. As parents, we must recognize that behind the allure of screens and social media lies a spiritual attack on our sons' hearts and minds. It's a subtle yet powerful force that draws them away from the truth of God's Word and His calling on their lives. Therefore, our approach must be spiritual as much as it is practical. We must wage war in the spiritual realm to break these chains.

Prayers to Break the Spirit of Addiction

To break the chains of social media and digital addiction, we must engage in targeted and specific prayers. Begin by praying for the Holy Spirit's conviction over your son's life. Ask God to open his eyes to the areas where digital consumption has taken precedence over his relationship with God, his studies, and his well-being. Pray according to Ephesians 1:18, that "the eyes of [his] heart may be enlightened in order that [he] may know the hope to which He has called [him]."

Pray for a divine dissatisfaction with superficial engagement and a longing for meaningful, real-world relationships. Bind the spirit of distraction and confusion in Jesus' name. Pray using the authority given to you as a parent and believer, declaring the truth of Matthew 18:18: "Whatever you bind on earth will be bound in heaven, and whatever you loose on earth will be loosed in heaven."

Declare freedom over your son's mind, emotions, and spirit. Speak out Psalm 119:37, "Turn my eyes away from worthless things; preserve my life according to your word." Speak this verse over him daily, asking God to turn his eyes from the addictive pull of screens and toward the life-giving truth of Scripture. Reclaim his time, his focus, and his identity in Christ through these prayers.

Equipping Your Son with Spiritual Tools

Prayer is foundational, but equipping your son with practical spiritual tools is equally important. Encourage him to start each day with prayer and Scripture reading before turning to any digital devices. The Word of God is "alive and active, sharper than any double-edged sword" (Hebrews 4:12), and can pierce through the fog of addiction and distraction. Suggest a daily devotion or a Bible reading plan that aligns with his interests and encourages spiritual growth.

Teach him to take a digital Sabbath, a day of rest from all screens, to reconnect with God, nature, and family. Encourage him to use that time to engage in activities that nourish his soul, such as journaling, exercising, reading Christian literature, or participating in community service. Remind him of Jesus' example in Mark 1:35, where He often withdrew to lonely places to pray. Help him see the value of stepping away from the noise to hear the voice of God.

Breaking the Spirit of Comparison and Insecurity

Social media is a breeding ground for comparison, jealousy, and insecurity. As you pray, focus on breaking these spirits over your son's life. Pray specifically against the spirit of comparison that leads to envy and self-doubt. Declare Galatians 1:10 over your son, reminding him that he is not called to please people but God. Pray for his identity to be firmly rooted in Christ, not in the ever-changing metrics of likes, follows, and shares.

Encourage your son to replace the time spent on social media with activities that build his self-esteem and reinforce his God-given identity. Help him understand that his worth is not determined by online validation but by the unwavering love of his Heavenly Father. This understanding will empower him to resist the temptation of digital addiction and find fulfillment in God's purpose for his life.

Reclaiming Your Home from Digital Strongholds

Finally, pray to reclaim your home from digital strongholds. Anoint your home with oil, symbolizing the Holy Spirit, and pray over each room. Declare your home a place of peace, rest, and godly focus. Speak out Deuteronomy 6:5-9, emphasizing the command to love God with all your heart, soul, and strength, and to impress His commandments on your children. Pray that your home will be a place where God's Word is spoken, lived, and treasured above all else.

Ask God to help you as a parent set healthy boundaries and model balanced digital use. Pray for wisdom to discern the right time to engage and disengage from screens. Remember, this battle is not yours alone; it is the Lord's (2 Chronicles 20:15). Trust in His power to break every chain and set your son free from every form of bondage, including digital addiction.

Walking in Continuous Victory

Breaking the chains of digital addiction is not a one-time prayer; it is a daily spiritual battle. Stay vigilant in prayer, rooted in Scripture, and intentional in your actions. Encourage your son to build his identity on the solid rock of Christ, not on the shifting sands of social media. Remain steadfast, knowing that "He who began a good work in you will carry it on to completion until the day of Christ Jesus" (Philippians 1:6). Through prayer, practical guidance, and the power of the Holy Spirit, your son can walk in victory and freedom from the bondage of digital addiction.

Overcoming Peer Pressure: Praying for Godly Influence

Peer pressure is a potent force in the lives of teenagers. It can be a relentless, unseen hand pushing them toward choices and behaviors that may contradict their values and upbringing. For many teenage boys, the need to fit in, be accepted, or feel a sense of belonging can lead them into situations that foster spiritual compromise, emotional turmoil, and even physical danger. However, as parents and spiritual guardians, we are not powerless against this force. Through the power of prayer, we can seek God's intervention, positioning His divine influence against the pressures that seek to shape our sons negatively.

Recognizing the Spiritual Dimension of Peer Pressure

Peer pressure is more than just a social dynamic; it is a spiritual battle. The Apostle Paul reminds us in Ephesians 6:12 that "our struggle is not against flesh and blood, but against the rulers, against the authorities, against the powers of this dark world and against the spiritual forces of evil in the heavenly realms." Peer pressure, especially when it encourages ungodly behavior, is a manifestation of these spiritual forces that seek to divert our sons from their God-ordained destinies.

To pray effectively against peer pressure, we must recognize that our fight is not merely against societal norms or youthful tendencies but against spiritual forces that seek to conform our sons to the patterns of this world (Romans 12:2). The enemy knows that if he can influence the influencers, he can steer our sons away from God's path. Thus, our prayers must be bold, direct, and filled with authority to break these spiritual chains.

Praying for Divine Disconnection from Negative Influences

Begin by praying for divine disconnection from all negative influences. Ask God to expose every ungodly friendship or association that might be leading your son down a path of destruction. Pray specifically for a revelation of truth, that the Holy Spirit would open your son's eyes to see the true nature of these influences. This prayer aligns with Psalm 1:1-3, which talks about the blessed man who does not "walk in the counsel of the wicked or stand in the way of sinners or sit in the seat of mockers."

Declare in prayer that your son will no longer walk in the counsel of the wicked. Speak forth that every relationship not planted by God in his life would be uprooted (Matthew 15:13). Ask for God's intervention to sever ties with those who seek to pull him away from his purpose. Pray that the Holy Spirit would bring discomfort in any relationship that is not in alignment with God's will until it is broken off completely.

Praying for Godly Friendships and Mentors

While praying for disconnection from negative influences, we must also pray for godly connections to be established. Proverbs 13:20 tells us,

"Walk with the wise and become wise, for a companion of fools suffers harm." Pray that God would bring wise and godly friends into your son's life—friends who will encourage him, build him up in faith, and stand with him in times of trial.

Ask God to raise up spiritual mentors who will guide your son with wisdom and love. Pray for teachers, youth pastors, or older peers who will have a godly influence over him. Declare in prayer that God will send individuals who are full of the Holy Spirit and wisdom, just as Barnabas was to Paul—a spiritual encourager who saw his potential and helped him walk into his calling (Acts 9:26-27).

Pray specifically that your son's social circle will be saturated with those who seek after God's heart, and that he will be drawn to people who exhibit the fruit of the Spirit (Galatians 5:22-23). Ask for divine appointments and connections that will nurture his spiritual growth and challenge him to pursue righteousness.

Building His Identity in Christ Through Prayer

A critical aspect of overcoming peer pressure is helping your son build a strong identity in Christ. The enemy often uses peer pressure to target insecurities, self-doubt, and the need for approval. Pray fervently for your son to have a revelation of his true identity as a child of God. Declare scriptures such as 1 Peter 2:9 over him, affirming that he is "a chosen generation, a royal priesthood, a holy nation, God's special possession."

Pray against the spirit of fear and insecurity that often accompanies peer pressure. Bind the spirit of fear in the name of Jesus (2 Timothy 1:7) and release the spirit of power, love, and a sound mind over your son. Declare that he will not be conformed to the patterns of this world but will be transformed by the renewing of his mind (Romans 12:2). Ask God to help him see himself as God sees him, to be secure in his identity, and to have the courage to stand alone when necessary.

Using Spiritual Weapons to Fight Peer Pressure

Teach your son to use his spiritual weapons. Encourage him to memorize and declare God's Word when faced with temptation or pressure to conform. The Word of God is "the sword of the Spirit" (Ephesians 6:17), and it is a powerful weapon against the enemy's schemes. Pray that the Word of God will dwell richly in him (Colossians 3:16), providing him with the strength and wisdom to resist ungodly influences.

Encourage him to use prayer as his first line of defense. Pray for the Holy Spirit to prompt him to pray when faced with pressure, to seek God's guidance, and to rely on His strength. Pray for discernment so he can identify the subtle tactics of the enemy disguised as harmless fun or innocent friendship.

Pray that he will wear the "full armor of God" (Ephesians 6:10-18) daily—truth, righteousness, peace, faith, salvation, and the Word of God. Declare that he will not be swayed by the opinions or behaviors of others but will stand firm, rooted and grounded in God's truth.

Standing Boldly in God's Power

Overcoming peer pressure is not an easy battle, but it is one that can be won through the power of prayer and the guidance of the Holy Spirit. As you pray for your son, remember that you are engaging in spiritual warfare on his behalf. Be relentless in your prayers, trusting that God is at work even when you cannot see immediate results.

Know that every prayer is a seed planted in faith, and in due time, you will see a harvest of righteousness in your son's life. Stand firm, be bold, and continue to pray without ceasing, for the God who began a good work in your son will be faithful to complete it (Philippians 1:6). Trust that through your intercession, your son will rise above the pressures of this world and walk confidently in the purpose God has set for him.

Breaking the Spirit of Rebellion and Disobedience

Rebellion and disobedience often manifest in teenage years, becoming a significant spiritual battle for many Christian families. In the teenage phase, the pursuit of independence, identity, and belonging becomes crucial. However, when rebellion and disobedience grip the heart, they not only challenge authority but also open doors to spiritual oppression and bondage. As parents, the calling to break these chains through prayer and spiritual warfare is vital.

Recognizing the Roots of Rebellion: The Enemy's Agenda

Rebellion is not just a behavioral issue; it is a spiritual one. The Bible tells us in 1 Samuel 15:23, "For rebellion is like the sin of witchcraft, and arrogance like the evil of idolatry." This verse illuminates the gravity of rebellion — it is aligned with witchcraft, indicating that it's not merely about defiance but about engaging with spiritual forces opposed to God's authority. The enemy seeks to sow seeds of rebellion in the hearts of teenagers, knowing it can lead to greater spiritual destruction. Recognizing that the spirit of rebellion is often rooted in pride, rejection, fear, or past wounds helps in understanding how to pray strategically against it.

Praying Against the Spirit of Rebellion: Engaging in Spiritual Warfare

To effectively pray against the spirit of rebellion, begin by understanding that this is not a battle fought with mere words but with the weapons of spiritual warfare. As Paul reminds us in 2 Corinthians 10:4, "The weapons of our warfare are not carnal but mighty in God for pulling down strongholds." Here are strategic prayers and steps to engage in:

1. Declare God's Sovereignty Over Your Son's Life:
Start by affirming God's authority over your son's life. Pray boldly, proclaiming that your son belongs to God and that his life is under divine

control. Use Scriptures such as Jeremiah 29:11 ("For I know the plans I have for you, declares the Lord...") to declare God's purpose over him. Speak these words aloud daily, believing that God's Word has the power to shatter the chains of rebellion.

2. Break the Stronghold of Rebellion with the Blood of Jesus:
The Blood of Jesus is a powerful tool in spiritual warfare. Revelation 12:11 declares, "They triumphed over him by the blood of the Lamb and by the word of their testimony." Pray for your son's deliverance, applying the Blood of Jesus to break the spiritual chains of rebellion. Say, "By the authority of Jesus Christ, I plead the blood of Jesus over [son's name] and break every spirit of rebellion trying to control his mind, emotions, and actions. In Jesus' name, I declare freedom and deliverance!"

3. Command the Spirit of Rebellion to Leave:
Jesus has given believers the authority to cast out demons and evil spirits. Speak directly to the spirit of rebellion with the authority given to you by Christ in Luke 10:19: "I have given you authority... to overcome all the power of the enemy." Pray with conviction, "In the name of Jesus Christ, I command every spirit of rebellion and disobedience tormenting [son's name] to leave right now. You have no authority here! Go to the feet of Jesus and never return."

Rebuilding Godly Character: Nurturing Obedience through Love and Grace

While prayers break spiritual chains, nurturing a heart of obedience requires continuous cultivation of godly character. Rebellion often emerges when a teenager feels misunderstood, unloved, or unaccepted. Healing from rebellion must be accompanied by love and grace. Here's how to nurture your son's heart in the process:

1. Model Godly Submission and Obedience:
Your example matters. Show your teenage son what obedience to God looks like through your actions. As Paul writes in 1 Corinthians 11:1, "Follow my example, as I follow the example of Christ." When he sees you submitting to God's authority joyfully, he learns to understand obedience not as a restriction but as a pathway to blessing and freedom.

2. Encourage Open Communication and Confession:
James 5:16 says, "Confess your faults to one another, and pray for one another that you may be healed." Encourage your son to speak openly about his struggles with rebellion. Create a safe space where he feels comfortable sharing without fear of harsh judgment. Let him know that confession brings healing, and guide him to confess to God for deliverance.

3. Use Affirmation and Positive Reinforcement:
The Bible reminds us that "a gentle answer turns away wrath, but a harsh word stirs up anger" (Proverbs 15:1). Affirm your son's positive choices, no matter how small. Celebrate his steps toward obedience, and offer

positive reinforcement instead of criticism. Use words that build up rather than tear down, reinforcing his identity as a child of God.

Daily Affirmation and Confession: Renewing the Mind

The battle against rebellion involves the mind. Romans 12:2 instructs us to "be transformed by the renewing of your mind." Encourage your son to meditate on Scriptures that emphasize obedience, humility, and submission to God. Here are a few powerful declarations to incorporate:

- "I am a child of God, and I submit my life to His will."
- "I have the mind of Christ, and I reject every rebellious thought."
- "The spirit of rebellion has no hold over me; I am free in Jesus' name!"

Encourage your son to speak these declarations daily. These affirmations, based on Scripture, will begin to shape his thoughts and attitudes, transforming his mind and spirit.

Walking in Continuous Freedom: Trusting God for Ongoing Deliverance

Breaking the spirit of rebellion is not a one-time event but a continuous process. Regular prayer, confession, and encouragement are crucial in maintaining freedom. Trust God to complete the work He has started in your son. Remember Philippians 1:6: "Being confident of this, that he who began a good work in you will carry it on to completion until the day of Christ Jesus."

Continue to stand in faith, knowing that God's power is greater than any spirit of rebellion or disobedience. Celebrate the progress, however small it may seem, and maintain a posture of prayer, knowing that "the fervent prayer of a righteous person is powerful and effective" (James 5:16). God is faithful, and He will bring your son to a place of peace, obedience, and spiritual maturity.

Releasing Your Son from Negative Friendships and Associations

In today's world, where influences come from every corner of society, the friendships and associations your teenage son forms can profoundly impact his spiritual and emotional well-being. Proverbs 13:20 declares, "He who walks with the wise grows wise, but a companion of fools suffers harm." This biblical truth reminds us of the critical importance of the people we allow into our inner circle. For a teenage boy, friendships can either be a source of strength and encouragement or a gateway to destructive behaviors, spiritual bondage, and moral decline. As a parent, your prayers are vital in releasing your son from any negative friendships and associations that may hinder his spiritual growth or lead him into paths of unrighteousness.

Understanding the Power of Associations: A Biblical Perspective

In the Bible, we see many examples of how associations can either build up or tear down a person's faith and character. Consider Samson, whose downfall began with an unwise association with Delilah (Judges 16). Similarly, King Solomon, who began his reign with divine wisdom, eventually turned away from God due to his relationships with foreign wives who worshiped other gods (1 Kings 11:1-4). These examples illustrate that associations have the power to lead one either closer to God or further away from Him. For your son, friends who do not share his values or faith can subtly, yet powerfully, draw him into compromise, rebellion, or even spiritual bondage.

This is where your role as a prayer warrior becomes crucial. Your prayers can serve as a spiritual barrier that protects your son from harmful relationships and helps him discern God's will regarding his friendships. It's about standing in the gap and calling on God's divine intervention to sever any unhealthy ties that might be drawing him away from his God-given purpose.

Praying with Boldness: How to Stand in the Gap for Your Son

To effectively pray for the release of your son from negative friendships and associations, your prayers must be strategic, specific, and Spirit-led. Here are five powerful strategies to consider:

1. Declare Spiritual Discernment Over Your Son's Life:

Begin by praying for the gift of discernment (1 Corinthians 12:10) to be imparted upon your son. Ask God to open his spiritual eyes so he can clearly see the character and intentions of those around him. Pray that he will have the wisdom of Solomon to distinguish between friendships that are nurturing his spiritual growth and those that are leading him astray. Declare that he will no longer be influenced by peer pressure or deceptive appearances, but instead be guided by the Holy Spirit in choosing his companions.

2. Break Soul Ties and Unholy Alliances:
In the spiritual realm, relationships can create soul ties—spiritual and emotional bonds that are formed through close, intimate connections. Not all soul ties are godly; some can be damaging and oppressive. As a parent, take authority in Jesus' name to break any ungodly soul ties that have been formed through negative friendships. Pray specifically, naming individuals if you are aware of them, and command any unholy alliance to be severed by the power of the blood of Jesus. Declare freedom from any emotional manipulation, control, or spiritual bondage that may have taken root due to these associations.

3. Ask for a Divine Hedge of Protection:
Just as God placed a hedge of protection around Job (Job 1:10), pray for a divine hedge of protection around your son—one that guards his heart, mind, and spirit from negative influences. Pray that this hedge will be impenetrable to any ungodly friendships, and that it will repel individuals with harmful intentions or ungodly agendas. Ask God to station His angels

around your son to protect him from the schemes of the enemy, who may use peers to tempt him away from his faith or purpose.

4. Pray for Godly Friendships to Take Root:
Jesus modeled the importance of godly friendships in His relationship with His disciples. Pray that God will bring godly friends into your son's life who will encourage him in his walk with Christ. Ask for companions who will speak truth in love, hold him accountable, and inspire him to pursue righteousness. Pray for mentors, youth leaders, or peers who can provide positive role models. Declare that your son will be drawn to those who reflect Christ's character, and that he will be a source of light and encouragement to others.

5. Intercede for Transformation and Salvation of Negative Influences:
While it's essential to pray for your son's release from negative associations, remember that those friends may themselves be lost, hurting, or in need of Jesus. Pray for the salvation of those individuals who have negatively influenced your son. Intercede for a transformation in their hearts, that they would come to know the love of Christ and be delivered from their own chains of sin and darkness. Pray that if it is God's will, these individuals will be brought to the light and their relationship with your son will be renewed in a way that glorifies God.

Releasing Your Son into His Divine Destiny

Once you have prayed for deliverance from negative friendships, it is important to release your son into his divine destiny. Begin to speak life, purpose, and destiny over him. Declare Jeremiah 29:11 over his life, that God's plans for him are to prosper him, give him hope, and a future. Affirm that God has set him apart for greatness and that no weapon formed against him shall prosper (Isaiah 54:17). Encourage your son to find his identity in Christ, reminding him that he is a child of the Most High God and that his worth is not defined by the acceptance of others but by God's love and calling.

Walking in Victory: A Parent's Ongoing Prayer Journey

Remember, this is not a one-time prayer but an ongoing journey. Continue to pray and intercede for your son regularly, trusting that God is at work even when you cannot see it. Rejoice in small victories and maintain a heart of gratitude for the progress you observe. Encourage your son to keep his heart open to the Holy Spirit's leading and to seek God in all his relationships. Your persistence in prayer will set a foundation of faith, hope, and love that will guide your son throughout his life.

God is faithful, and He hears the prayers of a parent's heart. Keep pressing into His presence, trusting that He will do exceedingly, abundantly, above all you could ask or think (Ephesians 3:20). Through your prayers, you are paving a pathway of deliverance and divine destiny for your son.

Deliverance Prayers

1. Heavenly Father, in the mighty name of Jesus, I take authority over every spirit of addiction seeking to control my son. I bind and cast out any demonic influence of substance abuse, declaring freedom and deliverance by the blood of Jesus. Father, break every chain, every stronghold, and release him into your perfect will.

2. Lord Jesus, I stand in the gap for my son, renouncing every connection he has made with substances that are destroying his body and mind. I pray that your Holy Spirit will fill every void in his heart, replacing his cravings with a deep hunger for your presence. Set him free, Lord, and make him whole again.

3. Almighty God, I pray that you will remove every desire for drugs, alcohol, or any harmful substance from my son's heart. I declare that these cravings are uprooted and removed in the name of Jesus. Fill his mind with your peace, and guard his heart against every temptation.

4. Father, in the name of Jesus, I come against every spirit of dependency that is gripping my son's life. I speak life and restoration over his body and soul, declaring that he is not bound by these substances, but is liberated by the power of Jesus Christ.

5. Lord, I ask for your intervention, breaking every spiritual, emotional, and physical attachment my son has with substances that harm him. I plead

the blood of Jesus over his life and proclaim complete deliverance and restoration, trusting in your mighty power.

6. In Jesus' name, I come against the spirit of distraction and addiction to social media that has captivated my son's attention. I declare that his time and focus are being redeemed by the Lord, and that he is being restored to the path of righteousness and purpose.

7. Father God, I pray that every stronghold of digital addiction, whether it be through social media, games, or online content, is broken in my son's life. Give him the strength to disconnect from anything that seeks to steal, kill, or destroy his peace and joy.

8. Lord, I ask you to intervene and break the chains of dependency on social media that consume my son's mind and spirit. Teach him to find his worth and value in you, and not in the validation of likes, comments, or followers.

9. In the authority of Jesus Christ, I declare a divine reset in my son's digital habits. I ask for the grace to manage his time wisely, prioritizing your Word and his relationship with you over fleeting digital pleasures.

10. Almighty God, I speak deliverance over my son from any unhealthy attachment to digital devices. I ask that you renew his mind, focus his thoughts on what is pure and noble, and free him from anything that distracts him from your calling and purpose.

11. Heavenly Father, I pray for divine discernment for my son in choosing friends and companions. I ask that you surround him with godly influences and remove any person who seeks to lead him away from your will and purpose.

12. Lord Jesus, I take authority over every spirit of peer pressure that seeks to conform my son to the patterns of this world. I declare that he is not of this world, but belongs to you, and will stand firm in his faith, resisting every temptation to compromise.

13. Father God, I ask you to grant my son the courage to say "no" when faced with ungodly choices. Fill him with boldness and confidence to be a light among his peers, influencing them for your Kingdom rather than being influenced by them.

14. In the name of Jesus, I break every unhealthy soul tie or friendship that negatively impacts my son's spiritual walk. I declare that he is rooted in your love and surrounded by those who lift him up in prayer and godly counsel.

15. Lord, I pray for a hedge of protection around my son, shielding him from negative influences and deceptive friendships. I ask that you guide him to relationships that build his faith and strengthen his walk with you.

16. Father, in Jesus' name, I take authority over the spirit of rebellion and disobedience that tries to take root in my son's heart. I declare that this spirit has no place in his life, for he is a child of obedience, walking in your statutes.

17. Lord Jesus, I speak peace over my son's heart and mind. I ask that you remove any root of defiance or rebellion, replacing it with a spirit of humility and submission to your will.

18. Heavenly Father, I declare that my son will not follow the path of disobedience, but will seek after righteousness and your divine guidance. I bind every spirit of pride and stubbornness and cast them out in Jesus' name.

19. In the authority of Jesus Christ, I break the spirit of disobedience that seeks to separate my son from your presence. I declare that he will follow your commandments, honor you in all he does, and live a life pleasing to you.

20. Almighty God, I ask that you soften my son's heart, making him receptive to your correction and guidance. I pray for a heart of flesh, a spirit that desires to know you deeply, and a mind that submits to your perfect will.

21. Father, in the name of Jesus, I come against every toxic relationship or association that leads my son away from your light. I declare that he is set apart for your glory and released from all ungodly ties.

22. Lord Jesus, I pray that you will remove every negative friendship that does not align with your plans for my son's life. Grant him the wisdom to recognize harmful influences and the courage to walk away from them.

23. Heavenly Father, I declare that my son is surrounded by godly friendships that uplift, encourage, and strengthen his faith. I ask that you divinely orchestrate connections that will propel him toward his destiny in Christ.

24. In the authority of Jesus, I break every soul tie formed with individuals who do not align with your will for my son's life. I plead the blood of Jesus over his relationships, asking for complete healing and separation from what is not of you.

25. Almighty God, I pray for a spirit of discernment for my son, that he may know whom to trust and whom to avoid. Protect his heart from deceit and guide him to friendships that reflect your love, truth, and righteousness.

Chapter 4

Healing from Emotional Wounds and Trauma

Prayers for Inner Healing: Addressing Past Hurts and Pain

Every teenager carries a story, a journey marked by moments of joy and hardship. Yet, beneath the surface of your teenage son's smile or his silence, there may be deep-seated wounds—pains of rejection, betrayal, abandonment, or trauma that have scarred his young heart. As parents, we often address the external issues—behavior, habits, and friendships—but what about the internal battles that rage unseen? Healing from emotional wounds is crucial for spiritual and emotional wholeness.

Understanding the Nature of Emotional Wounds

Emotional wounds are like unseen scars on the soul, often caused by hurtful words, traumatic experiences, or feelings of neglect and abandonment. These wounds may manifest as anger, withdrawal, rebellion, depression, or a desire for acceptance in the wrong places. According to Proverbs 18:14, "The spirit of a man will sustain his infirmity; but a wounded spirit who can bear?" A wounded spirit is a burden too heavy to carry alone—it requires the healing touch of Jesus, the One who "heals the brokenhearted and binds up their wounds" (Psalm 147:3).

Recognizing these wounds in your son requires spiritual discernment and a compassionate heart. Ask God for insight to see beyond the surface behaviors to the pain that may lie underneath. Emotional wounds can stem from various sources—family conflicts, bullying, loss of a loved one, divorce, or even societal pressures. Your son might not always express his pain verbally; instead, it could manifest in anger, aggression, or even withdrawal. Therefore, it is essential to create an environment of openness and safety where he feels heard and understood.

The Power of Prayer for Inner Healing

The first step toward healing these wounds is through prayer—a deliberate, focused, and fervent communication with God. Prayer is not just a ritualistic utterance; it is a spiritual weapon that taps into the divine power of God. In Matthew 11:28-30, Jesus invites us to bring our burdens to Him, promising rest for our souls. In the context of your son's healing, prayer becomes the bridge between his pain and the peace God offers.

- Prayer of Revelation and Understanding: Begin by praying for God to reveal the root causes of your son's emotional pain. Ask the Holy Spirit to bring into light the hidden wounds and past traumas that may be affecting his present behavior and mental state. Pray as the Psalmist did, "Search me, O God, and know my heart; test me and know my anxious thoughts. See if there is any offensive way in me, and lead me in the way everlasting" (Psalm 139:23-24). This prayer invites God to search deeply, to bring revelation where there is darkness, and to expose wounds that need His touch.

- Prayer of Forgiveness: Many emotional wounds are linked to unforgiveness—towards oneself, others, or even God. Unforgiveness acts like a poison, spreading through the heart and mind, affecting every area of life. Lead your son in a prayer of forgiveness, releasing those who have hurt him. Remind him that forgiveness is not about condoning the wrong done but about setting his heart free from the prison of bitterness. Encourage him to pray, "Lord, I choose to forgive [name the person] for [specify the offense]. I release them into Your hands, and I ask for Your healing in my heart." This act of forgiveness aligns with Jesus' teaching in Matthew 6:14-15, where He emphasizes the importance of forgiving others to receive our healing and forgiveness.

- Prayer of Healing and Restoration: Speak prayers of healing over your son, declaring God's promises for wholeness and restoration. Use scripture-based prayers such as, "He sent out His word and healed them; He rescued them from the grave" (Psalm 107:20). Declare that Jesus, the Great Physician, is healing every wound and scar. Command every spirit of trauma, pain, rejection, and fear to leave in the name of Jesus. Proclaim over your son, "By His stripes, you are healed" (Isaiah

53:5). This is not just a statement but a declaration of faith that taps into the power of the cross.

- Prayer of Identity and Purpose: One of the most profound wounds a teenager can carry is an identity wound—a distorted understanding of who they are in Christ. Pray for your son to have a revelation of his true identity as a child of God. Speak life into his destiny, declaring that he is "fearfully and wonderfully made" (Psalm 139:14) and that God has a plan and purpose for his life (Jeremiah 29:11). Encourage your son to see himself through God's eyes, as a beloved child with unique gifts and a significant role in God's kingdom. Pray against every lie of the enemy that tells him he is worthless, unloved, or without a future.

- Prayer of Peace and Comfort: Pray for the peace of God, which surpasses all understanding, to guard your son's heart and mind in Christ Jesus (Philippians 4:7). Ask the Holy Spirit, the Comforter, to envelop him with divine comfort, calming every storm within his soul. Declare that God's peace will replace every anxiety, every fear, and every sense of unease. Remind your son that Jesus said, "Peace I leave with you; my peace I give to you. I do not give to you as the world gives" (John 14:27). Let him find rest in this peace, knowing that he is held securely in God's hands.

Engaging in Practical Steps to Support Healing

While prayer is powerful, pairing it with practical actions is vital. Create an environment where your son feels safe to express his emotions. Encourage him to journal his feelings, engage in healthy activities, and, if needed, seek godly counsel from a pastor or Christian therapist who understands the spiritual dimension of healing.

Introduce him to Bible stories of individuals who experienced God's healing, such as David, who found solace in God amid his emotional turmoil, or Elijah, who was comforted by God in his depression. These stories can serve as anchors for your son's faith, reminding him that God is always present, even in his most challenging moments.

A Journey of Healing Through Christ

Healing from emotional wounds is not an overnight process; it is a journey that requires patience, faith, and perseverance. But take heart in knowing that God is deeply invested in your son's wholeness. He is the God who "makes all things new" (Revelation 21:5) and promises to "give beauty for ashes" (Isaiah 61:3). Your prayers, combined with faith-filled action, can be the catalyst for deep, transformative healing in your son's life, enabling him to walk in the freedom and fullness that God has purposed for him. Keep praying, keep believing, and trust that God is at work, even when you cannot see it.

Overcoming Depression and Despair through God's Comfort

Depression is a shadow that has crept into the hearts of many teenagers today. It is an unseen force that silently oppresses, steals joy, and clouds hope.

Understanding Depression: A Spiritual and Emotional Battle

Depression is not merely a medical or psychological condition; it is a profound spiritual and emotional battle. The Bible makes it clear that the enemy comes "to steal, kill, and destroy" (John 10:10), and one of the most effective weapons he uses against young people is the spirit of heaviness, often manifested as depression. Teenagers, already navigating the turbulent waters of identity, belonging, and purpose, can be particularly vulnerable to feelings of hopelessness, inadequacy, and overwhelming sadness.

As a parent, it is crucial to understand that depression in your teenage son is not a sign of his weakness or failure, nor is it an indication that he lacks faith. Instead, it is a call to arms, a summons to spiritual warfare, where you wield the Word of God and prayer as your primary weapons to combat the enemy's attacks on his mind and spirit.

Acknowledging the Pain: The First Step to Healing

The first step in overcoming depression and despair is acknowledging the reality of your son's pain. Encourage him to express his feelings openly, whether through conversation, journaling, or prayer. Remind him that even Jesus experienced deep sorrow and anguish, as seen in the Garden of Gethsemane, where He said, "My soul is overwhelmed with sorrow to the point of death" (Matthew 26:38). Depression is not a foreign concept to God; He is intimately acquainted with suffering and understands the depth of human despair.

As you listen to your son, validate his feelings without judgment. Let him know it is okay to feel overwhelmed, confused, or sad. Emphasize that emotions are a part of his human experience and that God's love and presence are steadfast, even in his darkest moments.

God's Comfort: A Balm for the Weary Soul

The Bible is filled with promises of comfort and hope, especially for those who are suffering. In Isaiah 61:1-3, God speaks of binding up the brokenhearted, proclaiming freedom for the captives, and releasing from darkness for the prisoners. He promises to bestow on them "a crown of beauty instead of ashes, the oil of joy instead of mourning, and a garment of praise instead of a spirit of despair." This is the transformative power of God's comfort – to replace the heaviness with joy, despair with hope, and mourning with praise.

Begin to pray these scriptures over your son. Speak them out loud in your home and declare them over his life. There is immense power in the spoken Word of God. It is not merely a collection of ancient texts but a living, breathing force that pierces through darkness and brings light. As Hebrews 4:12 states, "The word of God is alive and active. Sharper than any double-edged sword." Utilize this weapon of comfort and healing in your son's battle against depression.

Inviting the Holy Spirit: The Divine Comforter

The Holy Spirit is called the Comforter for a reason (John 14:26). Invite the Holy Spirit into your son's situation. Teach him to call upon the Holy Spirit in his times of deep sorrow, confusion, or anxiety. Encourage him to be still and allow the Holy Spirit to minister to his heart. The Holy Spirit is not distant; He is ever-present and willing to bring peace that surpasses all understanding (Philippians 4:7).

Pray daily for the Holy Spirit to envelop your son with His presence, filling every dark corner of his mind with light. Ask for a fresh infilling of the Holy Spirit to renew his mind and transform his thoughts, replacing negative self-talk and lies of the enemy with God's truth. This is a supernatural process; it requires faith and patience, but the results can be life-changing. The Holy Spirit brings clarity where there is confusion and peace where there is chaos.

Engaging in Spiritual Warfare: Breaking the Spirit of Heaviness

Depression often comes with a spiritual component known as the "spirit of heaviness." This is an oppressive spirit that seeks to weigh down the heart and mind, making the person feel stuck in a cycle of negative thoughts and emotions. Isaiah 61:3 offers a divine remedy for this: the "garment of praise for the spirit of heaviness." Praise is a powerful tool that confounds the enemy and invites God's presence.

Encourage your son to praise God even when he does not feel like it. Help him understand that praise is not just an emotional response; it is a deliberate act of spiritual warfare. When we praise, we shift our focus from our problems to God's greatness. As Psalm 22:3 declares, God inhabits the praises of His people. When your son praises God in the midst of his struggle, he invites God's presence into his pain, and where God is, darkness cannot remain.

Make praise a daily practice in your home. Play worship music, sing songs of gratitude, and encourage your son to write his own psalms of praise. This act of defiance against the spirit of heaviness can break its hold and allow the light of God's joy to flood your son's heart.

Building a Foundation of Faith and Hope

Finally, help your son build a foundation of faith and hope. Depression often thrives in a climate of hopelessness, but as believers, we have a hope that is "an anchor for the soul, firm and secure" (Hebrews 6:19). Teach your son to meditate on scriptures that speak of God's faithfulness, love, and plans for his future. Verses like Jeremiah 29:11, which declares, "For I know the plans I have for you," and Romans 8:28, which promises, "In all things God works for the good of those who love him," can provide a solid foundation to stand on when everything else feels uncertain.

Encourage your son to memorize these scriptures, speak them out loud, and declare them over his life daily. Faith comes by hearing, and hearing by the Word of God (Romans 10:17). As he fills his mind with God's truth, the lies of the enemy will lose their power.

Resting in God's Comfort

Overcoming depression and despair in your teenage son is not an instant process; it is a journey. But take heart in knowing that God walks with you every step of the way. As you pray, speak God's Word, invite the Holy Spirit, engage in praise, and build a foundation of faith, you create an environment where God's comfort can flow freely and healing can begin.

God's comfort is not a fleeting feeling but an abiding presence. It is the assurance that, even in the valley of the shadow of death, God is with us (Psalm 23:4). For your son, this comfort can become his anchor, his strength, and his guide out of the darkness of depression into the light of God's love and peace.

Praying Against the Spirit of Fear, Anxiety, and Insecurity

The Battle Against Invisible Chains

Fear, anxiety, and insecurity are spiritual forces that grip many teenagers today, often holding them captive in a prison of emotional turmoil. In a world that bombards them with messages of inadequacy, fear of the future, and threats to their identity, it is vital to recognize that these are not merely psychological or social issues but are often spiritual battles. The Bible declares, "For God has not given us a spirit of fear, but of power and of love and of a sound mind" (2 Timothy 1:7, NKJV). Therefore, the presence of fear, anxiety, and insecurity in a young person's life can signify a spiritual attack that needs to be confronted with prayer and God's Word.

Understanding the Spiritual Roots

Fear, anxiety, and insecurity can stem from many sources — traumatic experiences, rejection, bullying, academic pressure, or the loss of a loved one. However, beyond these surface issues, there are often deeper spiritual roots. The enemy exploits these emotional wounds, whispering lies into the minds of our teenagers: "You are not good enough," "You will never amount to anything," "No one truly loves you." These lies, when believed, form strongholds that trap them in cycles of fear and self-doubt.

The Bible warns that the devil prowls around like a roaring lion, seeking whom he may devour (1 Peter 5:8). For teenagers, the lion often roars through the voices of fear and insecurity, paralyzing them from stepping into their God-given destinies. But we know from Scripture that this roaring lion has already been defeated by the Lion of Judah, Jesus Christ.

Therefore, as parents and spiritual guardians, we have the authority to stand in the gap and wage spiritual warfare on behalf of our sons.

Breaking the Spirit of Fear through Prayer and Scripture

To effectively pray against the spirit of fear, anxiety, and insecurity, it is essential to wield the Sword of the Spirit, which is the Word of God (Ephesians 6:17). Begin by declaring out loud scriptures that affirm God's power over fear:

- Isaiah 41:10: "Fear not, for I am with you; be not dismayed, for I am your God. I will strengthen you; I will help you; I will uphold you with my righteous right hand."
- Psalm 34:4: "I sought the Lord, and He heard me, and delivered me from all my fears."
- Philippians 4:6-7: "Be anxious for nothing, but in everything by prayer and supplication, with thanksgiving, let your requests be made known to God; and the peace of God, which surpasses all understanding, will guard your hearts and minds through Christ Jesus."

As you speak these scriptures over your son, you are not only declaring God's promises but also releasing spiritual power to dismantle the lies of the enemy. Encourage your son to memorize these verses, meditate on them, and speak them out loud whenever fear or anxiety begins to creep in. The Word of God is alive and active, sharper than any double-edged sword (Hebrews 4:12). It pierces through the darkness, cutting off the spiritual chains that bind our children.

Practical Steps to Pray Effectively

1. Cover Your Son in Prayer Daily:
Every morning, lay hands on your son, if possible, and pray for God's peace to saturate his mind and heart. Declare that no weapon formed against him shall prosper (Isaiah 54:17). Ask God to surround him with His angels and to fill him with the Holy Spirit, who is the Comforter and Counselor.

2. Use the Authority Given by Christ:
As a believer, you have been given authority over all the power of the enemy (Luke 10:19). Use this authority to command the spirit of fear, anxiety, and insecurity to leave your son in Jesus' name. Speak directly to these spirits, declaring that they have no place in your son's life because he is covered by the blood of Jesus.

3. Invite the Holy Spirit into the Battle:
The Holy Spirit is our helper and advocate. Pray that the Holy Spirit will reveal any hidden fears or lies that your son believes. Ask the Holy Spirit to replace these lies with God's truth and to give your son a spirit of boldness and confidence.

4. Anoint His Room and Personal Belongings:

Consider anointing your son's room and personal belongings with oil, symbolic of the Holy Spirit's presence. Pray that every corner of his room be filled with God's peace and that his belongings would be consecrated for God's purposes. Ask the Lord to cleanse the atmosphere of his space from any negative spiritual influence.

5. Encourage Your Son to Engage in Worship:
Worship is a powerful weapon against fear and anxiety. Encourage your son to play worship music in his room, to sing praises to God, and to spend time in worship. As he does so, remind him that God inhabits the praises of His people (Psalm 22:3). In worship, fear and anxiety cannot stand, for they are overwhelmed by the presence of God.

Understanding the Power of Community

In addition to prayer, surround your son with a strong Christian community. Encourage him to connect with a youth group or Christian friends who can pray with him and encourage him in his faith journey. The Bible says, "Two are better than one, because they have a good return for their labor: If either of them falls down, one can help the other up" (Ecclesiastes 4:9-10). A supportive community will help your son realize he is not alone in his struggles and will provide the necessary support to reinforce his deliverance.

Replacing Fear with Faith

Finally, remind your son that fear is a liar and that his identity is rooted in Christ, who calls him "beloved," "chosen," and "fearfully and wonderfully made" (Psalm 139:14). Speak life over him daily, encouraging him to see himself through God's eyes. Replace fear with faith by reminding him that God has a unique purpose for his life and that no weapon formed against him shall prosper.

Praying against the spirit of fear, anxiety, and insecurity is not a one-time event but an ongoing battle. However, with persistent prayer, faith in God's Word, and the authority given by Christ, you can guide your son toward spiritual freedom and emotional healing. Encourage him to walk in the truth of who he is in Christ and to trust in the God who loves him beyond measure. Fear may roar, but remember: it is no match for the Lion of Judah.

Restoring Joy and Peace in Your Son's Heart

Restoring joy and peace in your teenage son's heart is not just a parental desire; it is a divine mandate. God created every human being to experience the fullness of joy in His presence and the peace that surpasses all understanding. However, the teenage years often bring an onslaught of challenges—emotional upheavals, identity crises, peer pressure, academic stress, and exposure to a world filled with uncertainties and temptations. These challenges can rob a young person of their God-given peace and joy. But as a parent, you have the spiritual authority and the divine assignment to intercede for your son, calling forth the restoration of his joy and peace through fervent, faith-filled prayer.

Understanding the Sources of Joy and Peace

To restore joy and peace, it is vital first to understand their true sources. According to the Bible, joy is not simply an emotion or a fleeting feeling; it is a fruit of the Spirit (Galatians 5:22). True joy is rooted in a relationship with Jesus Christ, who is the source of eternal gladness and satisfaction. Psalm 16:11 declares, "You make known to me the path of life; you will fill me with joy in your presence, with eternal pleasures at your right hand." This verse highlights that joy is a divine gift that comes from being in God's presence.

Peace, similarly, is not merely the absence of conflict or worry; it is a state of inner tranquility granted by the Holy Spirit. Jesus Christ, referred to as the "Prince of Peace" (Isaiah 9:6), offers a peace that is unlike any the world can give (John 14:27). This peace transcends circumstances, guards the heart and mind (Philippians 4:7), and is an anchor for the soul amid life's storms. Understanding these sources is crucial as you pray for your son because it shifts your focus from temporary solutions to God's eternal promises.

Identifying the Barriers to Joy and Peace in Your Son's Life

Before we can pray effectively for the restoration of joy and peace, it is important to identify the potential barriers in your son's life that may be obstructing these divine gifts. These barriers might include:

- Unresolved Sin and Guilt: Sin creates a separation between us and God, which can lead to a loss of joy and peace. If your son is struggling with hidden sin or guilt, he may feel a constant burden that drains his joy and fills him with anxiety.

- Negative Thought Patterns: The enemy often attacks through the mind, planting seeds of doubt, fear, insecurity, and hopelessness. Your son may be battling with negative self-talk, feeling unworthy, unloved, or inadequate, which steals his peace.

- Emotional Wounds and Unforgiveness: Past hurts, disappointments, and emotional wounds can create bitterness and a lack of peace. If your son is holding on to unforgiveness or is wounded by someone's actions, this can become a foothold for the enemy.

- External Influences: Ungodly influences, such as negative friendships, inappropriate media consumption, and worldly ideologies, can disrupt his spiritual equilibrium, drawing him away from God's peace and joy.

- Spiritual Attack: Recognize that there is a spiritual battle over your son's soul. The enemy comes to steal, kill, and destroy (John 10:10), and he targets young people with spiritual attacks aimed at their joy and peace.

Strategic Prayers for Restoration

To restore joy and peace in your son's heart, your prayers must be strategic, bold, and rooted in God's Word. Below are powerful prayer strategies to consider:

1. Pray for Repentance and Forgiveness:
Begin by praying that the Holy Spirit will convict your son of any sin that needs to be confessed and repented of. Ask God to reveal hidden sins and grant your son the grace to turn away from them. Pray for a spirit of repentance to fill his heart, and declare the cleansing power of the blood of Jesus over his life. Remember 1 John 1:9: "If we confess our sins, he is faithful and just to forgive us our sins and to cleanse us from all unrighteousness."

2. Pray Against Negative Thoughts and Lies:
Stand in spiritual warfare against the enemy's lies and negative thought patterns that may be infiltrating your son's mind. Take authority over every thought that exalts itself against the knowledge of God and command it to come into obedience to Christ (2 Corinthians 10:5). Pray specifically against fear, anxiety, self-doubt, and hopelessness. Declare that your son will have the mind of Christ (1 Corinthians 2:16) and that his thoughts will be aligned with God's truth.

3. Pray for Inner Healing and Emotional Restoration:

Call upon the Lord to heal any emotional wounds that may be hindering your son's joy and peace. Use Isaiah 61:1-3 as a foundation for your prayer, asking God to bind up the brokenhearted and to set free those who are captive to past hurts. Pray for the release of a spirit of forgiveness in your son's heart, that he may forgive those who have hurt him and experience the healing balm of the Holy Spirit.

4. Pray for Godly Influences and Discernment:

Intercede for godly influences to surround your son—mentors, friends, and leaders who will speak life, truth, and encouragement. Pray that he will have the discernment to recognize and reject ungodly influences. Ask God to give him wisdom to make choices that align with God's will, and declare that he will walk in the counsel of the godly (Psalm 1:1-3).

5. Pray for the Manifestation of the Fruit of the Spirit:

Pray specifically for the manifestation of joy and peace in your son's life as the fruit of the Holy Spirit (Galatians 5:22-23). Declare that the Spirit of God will fill his heart with joy and that he will experience a peace that surpasses all understanding. Ask the Lord to anchor your son in His love, that he may remain steadfast and unshaken by life's challenges.

Engaging in Warfare: Restoring What Was Stolen

Remember that prayer is not a passive exercise; it is an act of spiritual warfare. As you pray for the restoration of your son's joy and peace, take a stand against the forces of darkness that seek to steal these precious gifts. Declare boldly that your son belongs to the Lord and that every attempt of the enemy to rob him of his God-given inheritance will fail. Use scriptures as your sword (Ephesians 6:17) and speak them aloud, declaring the promises of God over your son's life.

Example Prayer:
"Father, in the name of Jesus, I come before you, standing in the gap for my son. I declare that he will not live in fear or anxiety, but in the peace of God that transcends all understanding. I rebuke every spirit of heaviness, depression, and despair. I ask you, Lord, to restore to him the joy of his salvation and to fill his heart with gladness in your presence. May your peace guard his heart and mind, and may your Spirit renew his thoughts and attitudes. In Jesus' mighty name, I pray. Amen."

Trusting in God's Faithfulness

Restoring joy and peace in your son's heart is not an overnight process; it requires perseverance, faith, and continual prayer. But take heart, for God is faithful. He desires your son's freedom even more than you do, and He will honor your prayers as you intercede in alignment with His Word. Stand firm, be bold in your declarations, and trust that the God of hope will fill your son with all joy and peace as he trusts in Him (Romans 15:13).

Your intercession has the power to change the atmosphere around your son, to reclaim what the enemy has stolen, and to restore him to the fullness of joy and peace that only God can provide.

Releasing Forgiveness and Breaking the Spirit of Bitterness

Forgiveness is a powerful and transformative act that transcends human emotions and reaches deep into the spiritual realm. For your teenage son, releasing forgiveness is not just an emotional decision; it's a divine mandate, a command from God that has the power to shatter chains of bitterness and resentment that may bind his heart.

The Spiritual Power of Forgiveness

Forgiveness is at the core of the Gospel message. When Jesus hung on the cross, He offered forgiveness to a sinful world, even to those who mocked Him in His final moments. "Father, forgive them, for they do not know what they are doing" (Luke 23:34). This profound act of grace sets the standard for all believers, including your son, to forgive others.

Forgiveness is not a sign of weakness or surrender; it is a declaration of spiritual authority. It is recognizing that vengeance belongs to the Lord and that only He can judge rightly. As a parent, it is crucial to impart this understanding to your son—that forgiving others is a step toward reclaiming his own freedom, healing, and wholeness. Forgiveness releases the hold of the enemy and opens the door for God's peace to flood his heart.

The Bible teaches that if we do not forgive others, God cannot forgive us (Matthew 6:14-15). This is a spiritual principle that cannot be ignored. The enemy will use unforgiveness as a foothold to torment and accuse, to stir up feelings of hatred and anger that can consume your son's mind. By releasing forgiveness, your son shuts the door to the enemy's schemes and allows the Holy Spirit to work deeply within him.

Understanding the Destructive Nature of Bitterness

Bitterness is a poison that slowly destroys from the inside out. It often begins with a small offense—a word spoken in anger, a betrayal by a friend, or a perceived injustice. Left unchecked, this seed of bitterness can grow into a massive root that entangles every area of your son's life. Hebrews 12:15 warns, "See to it that no one falls short of the grace of God and that no bitter root grows up to cause trouble and defile many."

Bitterness does not just affect the person who harbors it; it spreads like a virus to everyone around. It colors perceptions, distorts relationships, and can even impact physical health. Scientific studies have shown that prolonged bitterness can lead to high blood pressure, weakened immune function, and mental health issues such as anxiety and depression.

Spiritually, bitterness creates a barrier between your son and God, hindering his prayers and blocking the flow of God's blessings.

Bitterness is a spirit that the enemy uses to enslave God's people, particularly the young and impressionable. It deceives the heart into believing that holding onto anger or resentment will somehow punish the offender, but in truth, it is a prison in which the enemy wants to keep your son locked up. This is why breaking the spirit of bitterness is essential for his deliverance.

Praying for the Release of Forgiveness

Guiding your son to release forgiveness is a process that requires wisdom, patience, and most importantly, prayer. The act of forgiving is often a battle against the flesh—a wrestling match between human emotions and spiritual obedience. Here are several prayer points and strategies to consider:

- Pray for a Softened Heart: Begin by asking God to soften your son's heart. Ezekiel 36:26 says, "I will give you a new heart and put a new spirit in you; I will remove from you your heart of stone and give you a heart of flesh." Pray that God will replace any hardened areas in your son's heart with His tenderness and compassion.

- Pray for a Revelation of God's Forgiveness: Your son must grasp the depth of God's forgiveness toward him. Pray that the Holy Spirit would open his eyes to see the magnitude of God's grace, that he was forgiven much and, therefore, is called to forgive others (Matthew 18:21-35).

- Pray Against the Spirit of Bitterness: Use the authority you have in Christ to bind the spirit of bitterness and command it to leave in Jesus' name. Declare that your son will not be ensnared by this destructive force. Speak the Word of God over him: "Let all bitterness and wrath and anger and clamor and slander be put away from you, along with all malice. Be kind to one another, tenderhearted, forgiving one another, as God in Christ forgave you" (Ephesians 4:31-32).

- Pray for a Desire to Forgive: Often, the desire to forgive is not naturally present. Ask God to create within your son a desire to forgive, a longing for the freedom that comes from obedience to God's command. Pray that God would give him the courage to take the first step, even when it is painful or seems impossible.

- Pray for Complete Release and Healing: As your son begins to forgive, pray for complete healing of any emotional wounds caused by past hurts. Declare that he will not carry these burdens into his future, but will walk in the freedom Christ purchased for him on the cross. Pray for restoration in every area of his life—his mind, his emotions, and his spirit.

Breaking the Chains Through Forgiveness Exercises

While prayer is essential, practical steps should accompany spiritual warfare. Encourage your son to participate in exercises that help release forgiveness:

- Writing Letters of Forgiveness: Suggest that he writes letters to those who have hurt him, not necessarily to send, but to express his feelings and offer forgiveness. This act can be cathartic, helping him articulate and release his pain.

- Visualizing the Cross: Guide him to imagine placing his burdens, offenses, and unforgiven moments at the foot of the cross, releasing them to Jesus who has already borne all sins and sorrows.

- Daily Declarations: Encourage him to make daily declarations of forgiveness. For example: "In the name of Jesus, I forgive [name] for [offense]. I release them and bless them. I choose peace over bitterness."

- Seeking Counseling and Support: Sometimes, professional Christian counseling or speaking with a trusted pastor or mentor can help guide him through the process of forgiveness, offering additional tools and support.

- Regular Communion: Taking communion together as a family can be a powerful reminder of Christ's sacrifice and His forgiveness. This act reaffirms the covenant of grace and can help anchor your son in the reality of God's unending mercy and love.

Walking in the Freedom of Forgiveness

Releasing forgiveness is not a one-time event but a daily decision to walk in the grace that God has extended to us. Teach your son to forgive as a lifestyle, understanding that offenses will come, but he has the power to choose freedom over bondage. The process may be slow, and there may be moments of struggle, but every step toward forgiveness is a step toward victory, healing, and restoration.

By breaking the spirit of bitterness and embracing the power of forgiveness, your son can experience a life marked by peace, joy, and unshakable confidence in God's love. He will not only find freedom for himself but also become a channel of God's grace to others, demonstrating the heart of Christ in a broken world. This journey of forgiveness is not just about releasing others; it's about setting himself free to soar into the destiny God has prepared for him.

Deliverance Prayers

1. Heavenly Father, I come before you in the name of Jesus, asking for your healing touch upon my son's heart. Remove every wound of rejection, abandonment, and hurt that he has experienced. Fill the empty spaces in his heart with your unconditional love and peace.

2. Lord Jesus, I take authority over every memory that causes my son pain and command them to lose their grip on his mind and emotions. I declare that he is healed from past trauma, and no past event shall have power over his future.

3. Father, I break every word curse spoken over my son that has wounded his spirit and caused emotional pain. I declare in Jesus' name that those words are null and void, and I release life-giving words of affirmation, hope, and love over him.

4. Almighty God, I ask you to touch my son's mind and heal every thought that brings fear, insecurity, and self-doubt. Let your light shine in the dark places of his mind, bringing clarity, peace, and renewed confidence in who he is in Christ.

5. Lord, I declare that my son is free from all shame and guilt from his past mistakes. In Jesus' name, I release him from the bondage of regret, and I pray for the grace to forgive himself and move forward in your freedom.

6. Father God, in the mighty name of Jesus, I rebuke the spirit of depression and heaviness that weighs down my son. I command it to leave now, and I speak joy, peace, and the comfort of the Holy Spirit over his mind and heart.

7. Lord Jesus, you are the source of hope and life. I pray that you will pour out your joy into my son's life, breaking every chain of despair and hopelessness. Let him experience your presence in a powerful and uplifting way.

8. Heavenly Father, I take authority over every lie the enemy has whispered to my son that has led him to believe he is worthless or unloved. I declare in Jesus' name that he is precious, loved, and chosen by you.

9. Lord, I command the spirit of fear and anxiety to leave my son's life right now in Jesus' name. I declare that he shall not be overwhelmed by the cares of this world but shall rest in the knowledge that you are his strong tower and refuge.

10. Father, I pray that you replace every thought of despair with your thoughts of peace and a future. I declare that my son will find comfort in your promises and know that you have a plan and purpose for his life.

11. In the name of Jesus, I command the spirit of fear to be broken off my son's life. I declare that he shall walk in boldness and courage, knowing that you are with him wherever he goes.

12. Lord, I pray against every spirit of anxiety that seeks to overwhelm my son. I declare in Jesus' name that he shall not be anxious about anything but shall find peace in your presence and strength in your word.

13. Father God, I take authority over every insecure thought in my son's mind. I declare that he is secure in his identity as your child and that he is wonderfully made with a unique purpose and destiny.

14. Heavenly Father, I bind the spirit of intimidation and declare that my son will not be influenced by the opinions or judgments of others but will stand firm in his faith and confidence in you.

15. Lord Jesus, I pray for a divine exchange to take place. I release every fear, anxiety, and insecurity from my son's heart, and I ask that you fill him with your peace, courage, and assurance of your love.

16. Lord, in the name of Jesus, I speak restoration over my son's heart. I declare that every joy the enemy has stolen shall be returned sevenfold. Let the joy of the Lord be his strength and his portion forever.

17. Father, I pray that you will breathe new life into my son's spirit. Let your peace, which surpasses all understanding, guard his heart and mind in Christ Jesus.

18. In Jesus' name, I bind every spirit of sorrow and heaviness and release the spirit of joy, gladness, and celebration over my son's life. May he dance with joy in your presence and sing songs of praise.

19. Heavenly Father, I declare that my son's heart shall overflow with the peace that comes from knowing you. Let him be filled with a sense of calm, trust, and unwavering faith in your goodness.

20. Lord, I pray for supernatural joy to bubble up within my son's heart. May his laughter be a weapon against the enemy's plans, and may his joy be contagious to all those around him.

21. Father, in the name of Jesus, I pray for my son to have a forgiving heart. I ask that you help him release any unforgiveness he may hold against anyone, freeing him from the chains of bitterness.

22. Lord, I take authority over every spirit of resentment and declare it has no place in my son's heart. I release the love of God to flow through him, washing away all bitterness and pain.

23. Jesus, I pray that my son will experience the depth of your forgiveness for his own life, enabling him to forgive others easily and completely. Let your grace abound in his heart.

24. In Jesus' name, I break every stronghold of anger and unforgiveness in my son's life. I declare that he will not carry the weight of past hurts, but instead will be free to live in love and grace.

25. Lord, I ask that you fill my son's heart with compassion and empathy. Let him see others through your eyes and release any judgments or grudges he holds. May he walk in the freedom that forgiveness brings.

Chapter 5

Prayers for Spiritual Growth and Godly Character Development

Cultivating a Hunger for God's Word and Presence

In the journey of spiritual growth for a teenage son, one of the most crucial steps is to cultivate a deep and genuine hunger for God's Word and presence. This hunger is not a superficial desire, but a profound yearning that drives him to seek God above all else, transforming his heart, mind, and soul. As parents, it is essential to understand the importance of this hunger and to pray fervently for it to be ignited and sustained within your son.

The Foundation of Hunger: A God-Given Desire

To cultivate a hunger for God's Word and presence, we must first acknowledge that this hunger is divinely inspired. Jesus declared in Matthew 4:4, "Man shall not live by bread alone, but by every word that comes from the mouth of God." This hunger is not a natural inclination of the human heart; it is a supernatural gift from God, created by His Spirit to draw us closer to Him. For your son to experience this divine hunger, he needs an encounter with the Holy Spirit that opens his eyes to the reality and beauty of God's Word.

Begin by praying for a fresh encounter with the Holy Spirit in your son's life. Ask God to stir within him a dissatisfaction with worldly pleasures and pursuits, to the point where he finds them empty and unsatisfying. Pray that God will remove any spiritual dullness or apathy and replace it with a keen awareness of his need for God. This prayer is bold and dangerous because it invites God to disrupt comfort zones, but it is necessary for true spiritual growth.

Practical Prayers for Awakening Hunger

To awaken a hunger for God's Word, focus on specific prayers that target the heart and spirit. Here are some detailed prayers to guide you:

1. Prayer for Enlightenment and Understanding:
"Lord, open my son's eyes to see the beauty, depth, and power of Your Word. Remove every veil that blinds his understanding and ignite a deep love for Your truth. Let Your Word become alive and active in his heart, sharper than any two-edged sword, penetrating to divide his soul and spirit, joints and marrow (Hebrews 4:12). May he experience Your Word as the lamp to his feet and a light to his path (Psalm 119:105), guiding him in every decision and choice."

2. Prayer for a Thirst for Righteousness:

"Father, create in my son an unquenchable thirst for righteousness. Let him be like a deer that pants for streams of water, longing for You, O God (Psalm 42:1). May he seek first Your kingdom and Your righteousness, trusting that all other things will be added unto him (Matthew 6:33). Let him hunger for holiness, purity, and truth, rejecting all forms of wickedness and deception."

3. Prayer for Divine Encounters:
"Holy Spirit, I ask for divine encounters in my son's life that will awaken his spirit to the reality of Your presence. Speak to him in dreams, visions, and through Your Word. Let him feel Your nearness and know that You are real and alive. Surround him with Your love, so he may taste and see that the Lord is good (Psalm 34:8). Break every chain of doubt, unbelief, and indifference, and replace them with a passion for You."

Encouraging Consistent Engagement with God's Word

Cultivating a hunger for God's Word also involves encouraging consistent engagement with the Bible. Teenagers often face numerous distractions—social media, peer pressure, academic stress, and entertainment. To counter these distractions, create a spiritual environment that fosters daily interaction with Scripture. Encourage your son to start each day with a verse or passage that he can meditate on throughout the day.

Pray for discipline and focus in his daily routines. Ask God to give him a longing to return to His Word, even when he feels tired, overwhelmed, or uninterested. Invite your son to participate in family Bible study sessions where he can ask questions, share insights, and learn in a safe, supportive environment. Let these sessions be dynamic and engaging, using creative methods such as storytelling, visual aids, or role-playing to bring the Scriptures to life.

Overcoming Resistance to God's Presence

It's not uncommon for teenagers to resist spending time in prayer or Bible study, viewing it as boring or irrelevant. This resistance is often a reflection of spiritual warfare. Pray specifically against every spirit of distraction, confusion, and resistance that would seek to draw him away from God's presence. Declare with authority that no weapon formed against him shall prosper (Isaiah 54:17) and that every plan of the enemy to keep him spiritually disengaged is canceled in the mighty name of Jesus.

Consider fasting as a means to intensify these prayers. Fasting amplifies spiritual sensitivity and breaks strongholds that regular prayer alone may not address. Pray for your son's appetite for worldly things to diminish while his hunger for God increases. As you fast, declare Isaiah 58:6 over your son: "Is not this the fast that I have chosen: to loose the bonds of wickedness, to undo the straps of the yoke, to let the oppressed go free, and to break every yoke?"

Nurturing a Worshipful Heart

Finally, teach your son to cultivate a worshipful heart. Worship is more than just singing songs; it is a lifestyle of acknowledging God in all things. Encourage him to express gratitude daily, to praise God even in challenging situations, and to acknowledge God's sovereignty over his life. Pray for God to give him a heart of worship, one that delights in glorifying the Father.

Teach him the importance of quiet time before God, listening for His still, small voice. This can be nurtured by spending time in nature, journaling, or simply sitting in silence, reflecting on God's goodness and mercy. Pray that he would learn to recognize God's voice and respond with obedience and joy.

Inviting God's Fire

Ultimately, cultivating a hunger for God's Word and presence in your teenage son is inviting the fire of God into his life. It is a relentless pursuit of more of Him—a pursuit that requires patience, persistence, and passionate prayer. Trust that God, who began a good work in your son, will carry it on to completion until the day of Christ Jesus (Philippians 1:6). Keep praying, keep believing, and keep trusting that your son will become a man after God's own heart, driven by an insatiable hunger for His Word and His presence.

> Praying for the Fruit of the Spirit to Manifest in His Life

The Bible teaches us that the fruit of the Spirit is the visible evidence of God's transformative work within us. Galatians 5:22-23 lists these fruits as love, joy, peace, patience, kindness, goodness, faithfulness, gentleness, and self-control. For your teenage son, the manifestation of these fruits is crucial to his spiritual growth and character development. But how do we, as parents, pray for these attributes to flourish in his life? This subchapter explores this question with depth and intentionality.

Understanding the Fruit of the Spirit

The fruit of the Spirit is not a collection of desirable traits we try to develop through human effort alone; rather, it is the evidence of the Holy Spirit's active work in a believer's heart. For your teenage son, this means that these fruits will only manifest when he remains in communion with God and allows the Holy Spirit to mold and shape him. In John 15:4, Jesus says, "Abide in me, and I in you. As the branch cannot bear fruit by itself, unless it abides in the vine, neither can you, unless you abide in me."

Our role as parents is to pray fervently and specifically for the Holy Spirit to cultivate these fruits in our son's life, allowing him to live in alignment with God's will, even in the face of temptations, trials, and the tumultuous journey of adolescence.

Praying for Love: The Greatest Commandment

Begin by praying for love — not just any love, but agape love, the kind of unconditional love that mirrors God's own love for us. Pray that your son will experience this love first, understanding the depth of God's love for him, which will then empower him to love others without condition or expectation. Pray that his heart will overflow with love for God, his family, his friends, and even those who may oppose or hurt him.

Ask God to give him a heart that mirrors the love described in 1 Corinthians 13: patient, kind, not envious or boastful, not proud or rude, not self-seeking or easily angered, keeping no record of wrongs. Pray that this love will shape his relationships, guide his decisions, and anchor his identity in Christ.

Praying for Joy: Strength Amidst Trials

Next, focus on joy — not fleeting happiness dependent on circumstances, but a deep, abiding joy that comes from knowing Jesus Christ. Pray that your son will find his joy in the Lord, even in the most challenging moments of his teenage years. Ask God to help him see beyond the temporary pleasures of the world and discover the joy that comes from a relationship with Christ.

James 1:2-3 tells us, "Consider it pure joy, my brothers and sisters, whenever you face trials of many kinds, because you know that the testing of your faith produces perseverance." Pray that your son will learn to find joy not only in the good times but also in adversity, knowing that God is using every situation to build his faith and character.

Praying for Peace: Guarding His Heart and Mind

Peace is a precious commodity, especially in the life of a teenager bombarded by anxiety, peer pressure, and the demands of modern life. Pray for a peace that transcends all understanding, as described in Philippians 4:7, to guard your son's heart and mind in Christ Jesus.

Pray against the spirit of fear and confusion, and ask God to fill your son with a supernatural calmness, a sense of divine assurance that God is in control. Pray that he will learn to trust God with every aspect of his life, from his studies and friendships to his future, and that this trust will yield an unshakeable peace.

Praying for Patience: Waiting on God's Timing

Patience is a virtue often lacking in a world that demands instant gratification. Pray that your son will learn to wait on the Lord, trusting in His perfect timing. Pray against impulsiveness and rash decisions that could lead him away from God's path. Ask God to help him develop a spirit of patience that endures under pressure, as described in Romans 12:12: "Be joyful in hope, patient in affliction, faithful in prayer."

Pray that your son will learn to see delays not as denials but as opportunities for growth, to trust God more deeply, and to cultivate a mature faith that does not waver in uncertainty.

Praying for Kindness and Goodness: Reflecting God's Heart

Kindness and goodness are outward manifestations of an inward transformation. Pray that your son will be known for his kindness, extending compassion and grace to those around him, even when it is undeserved. Ask God to help him see others through the eyes of Jesus, to feel compassion for the hurting, to stand up for the marginalized, and to respond to needs with a heart full of mercy.

Pray also for goodness — a commitment to moral integrity and ethical living. Pray that your son will have a deep conviction to do what is right, even when it is difficult or counter-cultural. Ask God to strengthen his character, to make him bold in his stand for righteousness, and to lead by example, reflecting God's goodness in every aspect of his life.

Praying for Faithfulness: Standing Firm in Faith

Faithfulness is about commitment and perseverance. Pray that your son will remain steadfast in his faith, unwavering even when challenged. Pray that he will understand the importance of being faithful in small things so that he may be trusted with greater responsibilities (Luke 16:10).

Ask God to help him keep his promises, be reliable in his commitments, and grow in his spiritual disciplines, such as prayer, Bible study, and fellowship. Pray that his faith will be anchored deeply in the truth of God's Word, enabling him to withstand the trials and temptations that come his way.

Praying for Gentleness and Self-Control: Cultivating a Balanced Spirit

Finally, pray for gentleness and self-control. Gentleness is not weakness; it is strength under control. Pray that your son will embody this strength, responding to others with humility and grace, especially in conflict. Ask God to help him use his words to build up and encourage rather than to tear down.

Self-control is vital in a world that often promotes self-indulgence. Pray that your son will develop self-control in every area of his life — his thoughts, words, actions, and desires. Ask God to help him resist temptations, manage his impulses, and make choices that honor God. Pray that he will learn to say "no" to ungodliness and worldly passions and to live a self-controlled, upright, and godly life in this present age (Titus 2:12).

A Lifelong Journey of Growth

Praying for the fruit of the Spirit to manifest in your son's life is not a one-time event but a continuous journey. As a parent, remain steadfast in your prayers, believing that God is faithful to complete the good work He has started in your son (Philippians 1:6). Encourage your son to seek God daily, surrender to the Holy Spirit's leading, and trust that, in time, he will bear much fruit, bringing glory to God and fulfilling his divine purpose.

Prayers for Integrity, Honesty, and Righteousness

Integrity, honesty, and righteousness are not just virtues but foundational pillars upon which a godly life is built. As a parent, praying for your teenage son to embody these qualities is not merely an aspiration for good behavior; it is an intercession for his alignment with the heart of God. In a world increasingly marked by moral ambiguity and ethical compromises, your prayers can serve as a spiritual anchor, rooting your son in the unshakable truth of God's Word.

1. Understanding Integrity, Honesty, and Righteousness from a Biblical Perspective

Integrity is often defined as the quality of being whole or undivided, an unblemished state where actions align with convictions. Proverbs 10:9 states, "Whoever walks in integrity walks securely, but whoever takes crooked paths will be found out." This verse reveals that integrity is not merely about what one does in public but who one is in private. It is a steadfast commitment to truthfulness, regardless of circumstance or consequence.

Honesty, closely tied to integrity, is the unwavering adherence to truth. It involves a transparency of character where one's words, actions, and intentions are without deceit or falsehood. Ephesians 4:25 urges believers, "Therefore each of you must put off falsehood and speak truthfully to your neighbor, for we are all members of one body." Honesty is a reflection of God's own character; He is a God who "cannot lie" (Titus 1:2), and He calls His children to emulate this standard.

Righteousness, meanwhile, is the state of being morally correct and justifiable, aligning one's life with God's commands and standards. It encompasses both moral purity and the pursuit of justice, a longing to reflect God's holiness in every aspect of life. Matthew 6:33 declares, "But seek first His kingdom and His righteousness, and all these things will be given to you as well." Here, righteousness is seen as a priority for the believer, an essential pursuit that aligns one's life with the will of God.

2. Praying for Integrity: A Heart That Mirrors God's Wholeness

To pray for integrity in your son's life is to ask God to make him a reflection of His wholeness and perfection. Begin by declaring scriptures over your son, such as Psalm 25:21, "May integrity and uprightness protect me because my hope, Lord, is in you." As you pray, visualize the armor of integrity encircling him, guarding his heart against the temptation to compromise or conform to worldly standards.

Pray specifically against the pressures of dishonesty that often plague teenagers — the temptation to cheat on exams, to lie about their whereabouts, or to engage in deceitful behavior to gain approval. Ask the Holy Spirit to convict his heart whenever he faces these situations, empowering him to choose truth over deception.

Intercede for a heart that values transparency, praying that your son would understand that integrity is not about perfection but about authenticity before God and man. Pray for him to be sensitive to the Holy Spirit's prompting, quick to confess and turn from any action that breaches his integrity.

3. Praying for Honesty: A Spirit That Reflects God's Truthfulness

Honesty is a rare commodity in a world that often glorifies half-truths, white lies, and manipulation. Pray for your son to embody honesty in all his dealings. Begin by acknowledging before God the cultural and social pressures that often challenge young men to compromise their honesty — pressures to fit in, to exaggerate achievements, or to hide mistakes.

Pray for your son's words to be like "apples of gold in settings of silver" (Proverbs 25:11), valuable and pure, spoken with wisdom and truth. Ask God to place a guard over his mouth, to protect him from speaking words that do not align with His truth. Declare Colossians 3:9-10 over his life, "Do not lie to one another, since you have put off the old man with his deeds, and have put on the new man who is renewed in knowledge according to the image of Him who created him."

Pray that honesty would be woven into the very fabric of his being, not as a burdensome rule but as a natural outflow of a life committed to God. Ask for the courage to speak the truth, even when it's uncomfortable or unpopular, and for wisdom to navigate situations with grace and honesty.

4. Praying for Righteousness: A Life That Embodies God's Holiness

Righteousness is more than avoiding sin; it is a pursuit of God's holiness and a desire to live in a way that pleases Him. Begin your prayers by invoking God's righteousness over your son's life, asking the Holy Spirit to stir within him a deep hunger for God and a passionate pursuit of His righteousness.

Declare over him the promise of Matthew 5:6, "Blessed are those who hunger and thirst for righteousness, for they shall be filled." Pray that he would be dissatisfied with anything less than the fullness of God's righteousness, rejecting the counterfeits and empty pleasures that the world offers.

Pray for righteous friendships and influences to surround him, lifting him up rather than pulling him down. Intercede for his interactions, both online and offline, asking God to purify his conversations, habits, and choices.

Pray for a discerning spirit, one that can recognize the difference between the holy and the profane, the sacred and the secular.

Ask God to lead your son in paths of righteousness for His name's sake (Psalm 23:3), and to anoint him with the courage to stand for what is right, even when he stands alone. Pray that his life would be a testimony to others, a beacon of light and a testament of what it means to live in righteousness.

5. Equipping Your Son with the Word: Scriptures to Declare and Meditate Upon

Finally, equip your son with specific scriptures to memorize, declare, and meditate upon as he cultivates integrity, honesty, and righteousness:

- Psalm 15:2-3 - "The one whose walk is blameless, who does what is righteous, who speaks the truth from their heart; whose tongue utters no slander, who does no wrong to a neighbor, and casts no slur on others."
- Proverbs 12:22 - "The Lord detests lying lips, but He delights in people who are trustworthy."
- Psalm 119:9 - "How can a young man keep his way pure? By guarding it according to Your word."
- 1 Timothy 4:12 - "Let no one despise you for your youth, but set the believers an example in speech, in conduct, in love, in faith, in purity."

Encourage your son to personalize these scriptures, making them his own by turning them into prayers and declarations. Remind him that his character is not defined by the world but by the Word of God, and through prayer, faith, and obedience, he can walk in the fullness of integrity, honesty, and righteousness that God desires for him.

A Call to Action

As you engage in these prayers, remember that your intercession has the power to shape and transform your son's character. Be persistent, bold, and unwavering, trusting that God, who began a good work in him, will carry it on to completion until the day of Christ Jesus (Philippians 1:6). Your prayers are a mighty weapon in the hands of a loving parent — use them to build a fortress of integrity, honesty, and righteousness around your son's heart.

Encouraging a Life of Prayer and Communion with God

A life of prayer is not just an option but a necessity for every believer, especially for young people navigating the turbulent years of adolescence. As a parent, encouraging your teenage son to develop a vibrant prayer life is one of the greatest gifts you can offer.

The Power of Prayer: A Lifeline to the Divine

Prayer is the lifeline that connects us to the divine, an open channel through which we commune with the Creator of the universe. For a teenager, who may often feel overwhelmed by the pressures of school, friendships, and the search for identity, prayer becomes a sanctuary—a place where they can find peace, direction, and affirmation in a world full of noise and confusion.

Scripture is replete with examples of the power of prayer. From Daniel, who prayed three times a day even when threatened with death (Daniel 6:10), to David, who wrote psalms of heartfelt cries to God, prayer has always been the foundation for spiritual strength and resilience. As parents, it is crucial to teach your son that prayer is not just a religious ritual but a dynamic conversation with a loving Father who listens and responds.

Encouraging your son to pray is more than just teaching him to recite words. It is about nurturing a deep, personal relationship with God, one that is authentic, continuous, and transformative. This begins with modeling a life of prayer yourself, showing him that prayer is as vital as breathing, a spiritual practice that draws us closer to God and aligns our hearts with His purposes.

Strategies for Cultivating a Prayerful Heart

1. Modeling the Prayer Life:

The first and most effective way to encourage your son to develop a life of prayer is by modeling it yourself. Let him see you pray in both private and public settings, demonstrating that prayer is not just a Sunday activity but a daily discipline. Share with him the times God answered your prayers or brought comfort in difficult moments. When he sees the reality of prayer in your life, he will be more inclined to desire the same connection with God.

2. Creating a Prayer Routine:
Encourage your son to establish a regular time for prayer each day. This routine doesn't need to be rigid, but consistency is key. Suggest he starts his day by dedicating the first few minutes to God, thanking Him for His goodness and seeking His guidance for the day ahead. The morning prayer sets the tone for the rest of the day, anchoring his thoughts in God's Word and preparing his spirit for whatever comes his way. Encourage him to pray at night, reflecting on the day's events, confessing any known sins, and expressing gratitude.

3. Praying the Scriptures:
One of the most powerful ways to teach your son to pray is by using the Word of God itself. Encourage him to pray through the Psalms, using them as a guide to express his emotions and thoughts. For example, Psalm 23 can be a prayer of trust and reliance on God's guidance. Psalm 91 can be a declaration of God's protection. Praying the scriptures aligns our prayers with God's will and fills them with divine power, ensuring that they are according to His Word.

4. Encouraging Honest Prayers:

Help your son understand that prayer is not about using the "right" words or adopting a formal tone but about speaking honestly and openly with God. Encourage him to bring all his thoughts, feelings, doubts, and fears before God without fear of judgment. Remind him that God already knows his heart (Psalm 139:1-4) and desires an authentic relationship. Honest prayers build intimacy with God, allowing Him to heal wounds, provide clarity, and guide decisions.

5. Incorporating Prayer into Everyday Life:

Encourage your son to see prayer as a conversation that continues throughout the day. Help him understand that prayer doesn't always require a specific place or time—it can happen anywhere, anytime. Suggest he prays while walking to school, before a test, or when facing a challenge with friends. Teach him the habit of whispering quick prayers—sometimes called "breath prayers"—such as "Lord, give me strength" or "Jesus, be with me now." This practice reinforces the reality that God is ever-present and interested in every detail of his life.

Breaking Through Spiritual Resistance

Teenagers often face spiritual resistance when it comes to prayer. They may feel awkward, embarrassed, or even disinterested. As a parent, you can pray against any spirit of resistance or apathy. Use your authority in

Christ to bind the spirit of distraction, discouragement, or doubt that might hinder your son from engaging with God.

Pray for a supernatural hunger for God's presence to fill his heart. Ask the Holy Spirit to give him a desire to know God intimately, to experience His love, and to hear His voice. Declare that your son will grow in his passion for prayer and that no weapon formed against his spiritual development will prosper (Isaiah 54:17).

Prayer for Your Son: Fostering a Life of Communion with God

"Father, in the name of Jesus, I thank you for my son. I thank you for the unique and wonderful person you have created him to be. I pray that you stir within him a deep hunger and thirst for your presence. Let his heart be drawn to you, Lord, in a way that cannot be quenched by the things of this world.

Holy Spirit, teach him how to pray, to seek you with all his heart, mind, and soul. Remove any resistance, doubt, or fear that may prevent him from experiencing the joy and peace of communion with you. Surround him with your love, and help him understand that you are always near, listening, and ready to guide him through every challenge.

Lord, I ask that you give him the discipline to cultivate a daily habit of prayer, to seek your face early in the morning and late in the night. May he find comfort and strength in your presence. I declare that my son will grow in spiritual wisdom, discernment, and faith, and that he will walk closely with you all the days of his life. In Jesus' mighty name, Amen."

A Journey Toward God's Heart

Encouraging your teenage son to live a life of prayer is an ongoing journey. It involves patience, perseverance, and constant intercession. Remember, you are sowing seeds that will bear fruit in due season. Trust that God, who began a good work in your son, will carry it on to completion (Philippians 1:6). Keep praying, keep encouraging, and most importantly, keep believing that through prayer, your son will discover the incredible adventure of walking hand in hand with God.

Building Faith to Stand Firm Against Temptations

In the journey of raising a teenage son, few challenges are as significant as preparing him to stand firm against the countless temptations he will face. In a world filled with enticements that appeal to every sense and emotion, from social pressures to moral compromises, equipping him with unwavering faith is essential. As a parent, you have a divine responsibility to help your son develop a faith that not only endures but thrives in the face of trials. This faith is not merely intellectual assent but a dynamic, living trust in God that fortifies him against the lures of the world, the flesh, and the devil.

1. Understanding the Nature of Temptations

Temptation is not sin; rather, it is the invitation to sin. Jesus Himself was tempted in every way as we are, yet without sin (Hebrews 4:15). This truth should bring immense comfort. It reassures us that temptation is a common human experience, not an isolated assault. But it also underscores the importance of preparing our sons to recognize and resist temptation before it leads to sin. The enemy knows your son's vulnerabilities, his weaknesses, and the areas where he is most likely to stumble. Like a roaring lion, Satan prowls around, seeking whom he may devour (1 Peter 5:8).

Therefore, building faith in your son involves teaching him to recognize the subtle and overt forms of temptation he will encounter — temptations of the eyes (lust, materialism), temptations of the flesh (sexual immorality, addiction), and temptations of pride (self-reliance, rebellion). Understanding the nature of these temptations empowers him to stand firm.

2. Grounding in the Word of God: The Sword of the Spirit

To build faith, you must immerse your son in the Word of God. Faith comes by hearing and hearing by the Word of Christ (Romans 10:17). The Word is not just knowledge; it is the sword of the Spirit (Ephesians 6:17) — the offensive weapon in the armor of God. Teach your son that every word in the Bible is God-breathed, profitable for teaching, rebuking, correcting, and training in righteousness (2 Timothy 3:16).

Encourage him to memorize Scripture, especially verses that pertain to standing firm against temptation. For example, Psalm 119:9-11, "How can a young man keep his way pure? By living according to Your word. I seek You with all my heart; do not let me stray from Your commands. I have hidden Your word in my heart that I might not sin against You." When temptations arise, these Scriptures will become like arrows in his quiver, ready to be deployed in the heat of battle.

3. Cultivating a Prayerful Life: Communing with God

A vibrant prayer life is essential in building faith that withstands temptation. Prayer is not a monologue but a dialogue with God, where your son can bring his fears, doubts, and struggles before the throne of grace and receive mercy and find grace to help in his time of need (Hebrews 4:16). Encourage your son to make prayer his first response, not his last resort.

Model this for him by praying with him and for him. Teach him the importance of praying "without ceasing" (1 Thessalonians 5:17) — of maintaining an ongoing conversation with God throughout the day. Guide him to pray specific prayers, like those Jesus taught: "Lead us not into temptation, but deliver us from evil" (Matthew 6:13). Praying this prayer isn't a sign of weakness; it's a declaration of dependence on God's strength and protection.

4. Fostering an Accountability Network: Strength in Community

Your son must not fight alone. God has designed us to live in community, to bear one another's burdens, and so fulfill the law of Christ (Galatians 6:2). Encourage him to build a network of godly mentors, peers, and friends who will support him in his faith journey. These relationships serve as both a safety net and a source of strength.

Accountability partners provide the wisdom, correction, encouragement, and prayer support that is crucial in times of temptation. Help your son find a youth group, a discipleship program, or a small group where he can connect with other believers who are committed to walking in purity and righteousness. Teach him that "as iron sharpens iron, so one person sharpens another" (Proverbs 27:17). In such relationships, he can experience the love and grace of God through the encouragement and support of others.

5. Embracing the Power of the Holy Spirit: Divine Empowerment

Finally, teach your son to rely on the power of the Holy Spirit. The Holy Spirit is our Comforter, Helper, and Guide, who empowers us to overcome the works of the flesh (Galatians 5:16-25). Encourage your son to seek the baptism and the continual infilling of the Holy Spirit (Ephesians 5:18), which empowers him to live victoriously in Christ.

Teach him that he is not alone in his struggles. The Spirit of God who raised Jesus from the dead dwells in him, and greater is He who is in him than he who is in the world (1 John 4:4). Encourage him to listen to the voice of the Spirit, who leads him away from temptation and gives him the courage to say "No" to ungodliness and worldly passions (Titus 2:12).

Encourage your son to walk by the Spirit, recognizing that it is not by his might nor by his power, but by God's Spirit that he will prevail (Zechariah 4:6). The Holy Spirit enables him to resist the devil, who must flee when confronted by someone clothed in the righteousness and authority of Christ (James 4:7).

Standing Firm in Faith — A Lifelong Journey

Building faith to stand firm against temptation is not a one-time event but a lifelong journey. It requires continual effort, trust in God, immersion in His Word, a commitment to prayer, active participation in a faith community, and a dependence on the Holy Spirit's power. As you guide your son on this path, remember that God is faithful, and He will not allow your son to be tempted beyond what he can bear (1 Corinthians 10:13). With every temptation, He will also provide a way out so that he can endure it.

Encourage your son that even if he stumbles, God's grace is sufficient. Help him understand that the righteous may fall seven times, but they rise again (Proverbs 24:16). Keep reminding him of God's steadfast love and the victory that is already his in Christ Jesus.

Through these steps, you will help him cultivate a faith that is unshakeable, rooted deeply in the love and truth of God, and capable of standing firm against any temptation the enemy may throw his way.

Deliverance Prayers

1. Heavenly Father, I pray that you ignite a deep and insatiable hunger in my son's heart for your Word. Let him crave the truth and wisdom found in the Scriptures, turning to you as his source of guidance, strength, and knowledge. May your Word be a lamp to his feet and a light to his path, drawing him closer to your presence each day.

2. Lord Jesus, remove every distraction that hinders my son from spending time with you. Open his eyes to the joy and peace that comes from a life devoted to prayer and communion with you. Let him find true satisfaction only in your presence, seeking you early and often.

3. Holy Spirit, breathe fresh life into my son's spirit. I ask that you stir within him a desire to know you more intimately. Let his heart burn with passion for your presence, and may he find rest and comfort in your embrace. Fill him with an awareness of your nearness at all times.

4. Father, I declare that my son's heart will not be drawn to worldly pleasures but will be rooted in a love for your Word. Place a yearning within him for spiritual growth, a thirst for righteousness, and a commitment to seek first your Kingdom and righteousness above all else.

5. Lord, I ask that you plant within my son a desire for godly knowledge and understanding. Cause him to pursue wisdom, and to be diligent in his study of your Word. May your truths penetrate his heart and transform his mind, renewing him day by day.

6. Heavenly Father, I pray that your Holy Spirit will develop in my son the fruit of love, allowing him to love others with a Christlike love, selfless and unconditional. Let his life be a reflection of your love in all he does and says.

7. Lord, I speak peace over my son's heart and mind, casting out anxiety, fear, and confusion. Let the fruit of peace manifest in his spirit, creating calmness amid chaos, and a sense of serenity that surpasses all understanding.

8. Holy Spirit, I pray that you fill my son with joy unspeakable and full of glory. Let your joy become his strength, even in times of difficulty and trial. May he find his greatest delight in your presence and your promises.

9. Father, I declare that my son will exhibit patience in all circumstances. Help him to trust in your perfect timing and purpose for his life. Teach him to wait upon you, knowing that your plans for him are good and full of hope.

10. Lord Jesus, I pray that my son will be a reflection of your kindness and goodness. Let his actions and words be filled with compassion and mercy toward others, demonstrating the love of Christ in tangible ways.

11. Father, I pray that my son will walk in integrity all the days of his life. Let his heart be pure and his actions be righteous, rejecting deceit and dishonesty in all forms. May he live in a way that is pleasing to you, honoring your name in everything he does.

12. Lord, I speak truth over my son's life. Let him be a lover of truth, rejecting lies and falsehood. Help him to stand for what is right, even when it is difficult, and to speak truth with courage and conviction.

13. Holy Spirit, guide my son to make decisions that reflect your righteousness. Let him be known for his honesty, uprightness, and fairness in all his dealings. May his life be a testimony of your character and a witness to your transforming power.

14. Jesus, I pray that my son will have a heart that is quick to repent when he falls short and quick to forgive those who wrong him. Let his life be marked by a pursuit of holiness and a desire to be right with you.

15. Father, I declare that my son will live according to your Word, rejecting the ways of the world. Give him the strength to resist temptation and the wisdom to choose the path of righteousness always.

16. Lord Jesus, I pray that my son will develop a strong and unshakeable prayer life. Let him come to you with all his concerns, knowing that you hear and answer. Teach him to trust in the power of prayer and to find refuge in your presence.

17. Holy Spirit, I ask that you draw my son into deeper fellowship with you. Let prayer be his first response in every situation, not his last resort. May he learn to pray without ceasing, keeping his mind and heart focused on you.

18. Father, I pray that my son will experience the joy and peace that comes from a consistent prayer life. Teach him to listen to your voice and to recognize your guidance in every area of his life.

19. Lord, help my son to build a habit of daily communion with you. Let him find strength in your presence, encouragement in your Word, and guidance in your Spirit. May he become a prayer warrior, standing firm in faith and intercession.

20. Jesus, I declare that my son will seek you in prayer, not just for his own needs but for the needs of others. Teach him the value of intercessory prayer and give him a heart that is burdened for your people.

21. Heavenly Father, I pray that you strengthen my son's faith, enabling him to resist every temptation that comes his way. Let him put on the full armor of God, standing firm against the schemes of the enemy.

22. Lord, I ask that you protect my son from the traps of the evil one. Grant him discernment to recognize temptation and the wisdom to flee from it. May he hold fast to your Word as his shield and sword in battle.

23. Holy Spirit, I declare that my son will not be overcome by the lusts of the flesh, the lust of the eyes, or the pride of life. Give him a deep conviction to live a holy life, pleasing unto you.

24. Jesus, I pray that my son will find his identity and worth in you alone, rejecting the lies of the world. Strengthen his resolve to live according to your standards, not succumbing to peer pressure or worldly desires.

25. Father, I speak victory over my son's life. He will overcome every temptation by the power of your Spirit. Let him be grounded in faith, confident in your promises, and unwavering in his commitment to follow you all his days.

Chapter 6

Overcoming the Spirit of Rebellion and Disobedience

Breaking the Spirit of Pride and Stubbornness

In the journey of raising a teenage son, parents often face the daunting challenge of dealing with pride and stubbornness. These traits, while sometimes appearing as mere parts of growing up, can often signal deeper spiritual issues that need to be addressed with spiritual discernment and authority. From a Christian perspective, pride and stubbornness are not just personality flaws or teenage angst; they can be manifestations of a spirit of rebellion, a condition that can lead to greater spiritual bondage if left unaddressed.

Understanding the Spirit of Pride and Stubbornness

The Bible speaks clearly about the dangers of pride. Proverbs 16:18 warns, "Pride goes before destruction, a haughty spirit before a fall." Pride is more than just an inflated sense of self; it is a spiritual condition that exalts itself against the knowledge of God (2 Corinthians 10:5). Stubbornness, closely related to pride, is the refusal to change one's attitude or position, even in the face of truth or authority. In 1 Samuel 15:23, the Bible equates stubbornness with idolatry, placing it on the same level as a rebellious spirit.

The spirit of pride and stubbornness often manifests in teenagers through defiance, refusal to listen to parental guidance, rejection of authority, and an exaggerated sense of independence. While it is natural for teenagers to seek autonomy, pride and stubbornness take this quest to a spiritually dangerous place, leading them away from God's purpose and protection. Recognizing this behavior as a spiritual battle rather than just a phase is the first step in combating it effectively.

The Root Causes of Pride and Stubbornness

To break the spirit of pride and stubbornness, one must first understand its root causes. Often, these traits can stem from several sources:

- Wounds and Insecurity: Many teenagers adopt a stance of pride and stubbornness to mask deeper emotional wounds or insecurities. A son who feels unworthy, unloved, or rejected may put on a façade of arrogance or resistance to protect himself from further hurt.

- Influence of Peers and Culture: The culture surrounding teenagers today often glorifies self-reliance, rebellion against authority, and a 'me-first' mentality. Influences from peers, social media, and entertainment can subtly (or overtly) encourage behaviors that align with the spirit of pride and stubbornness.

- Generational Patterns: Sometimes, pride and stubbornness can be generational strongholds passed down through family lines. If there is a history of rebellion or pride in the family, this spirit can manifest more strongly in the teenage years, where identity and independence are being actively shaped.

- Spiritual Attacks: As parents, it is crucial to remember that there is a spiritual war raging over your son's life. The enemy seeks to establish footholds in areas like pride and stubbornness to draw him away from God's purpose. Recognizing this spiritual reality enables parents to engage in targeted, effective prayer.

Praying to Break the Spirit of Pride and Stubbornness

Prayer is the most powerful tool in the battle against the spirit of pride and stubbornness. Here are specific prayers and declarations you can use to break these spirits:

- Prayer of Repentance and Renunciation: Begin with a prayer of repentance on behalf of your son. Even though he must ultimately repent for himself, as a parent, you stand in the gap and intercede for his spiritual freedom. Pray:

- "Heavenly Father, I come before You in repentance for any spirit of pride and stubbornness that has taken root in my son's heart. I renounce any generational patterns of pride, rebellion, and idolatry that may be influencing him. I declare that pride and stubbornness have no place in his life, in Jesus' name."

- Prayer for a Humble Heart: Pray that God will soften your son's heart, removing any stony areas and replacing them with a heart of flesh (Ezekiel 36:26). Ask God to instill in him a spirit of humility and teachability. Pray:

  "Lord, I ask that You remove any hardness of heart from my son and replace it with a heart that is tender and responsive to Your Spirit. Give him a teachable spirit and a desire to walk in humility, submitting to Your will above all else."

- Declaring Scripture Over Your Son: Speak the Word of God over your son's life. Declare James 4:6, "God opposes the proud but gives grace to the humble." Pray that your son receives the grace of humility and resists the temptation to elevate himself above others or God.

- Warfare Prayer Against the Spirit of Rebellion: Engage in spiritual warfare by taking authority over the spirit of pride and stubbornness in your son's life. Pray:

"In the name of Jesus, I take authority over every spirit of pride and rebellion that seeks to influence my son. I bind and break the hold of these spirits over his life. I command you to loose your grip and leave him now, in Jesus' name. He is marked by the blood of Jesus and belongs to God."

- Praying for a Spirit of Wisdom and Revelation: Ask God to reveal His truth to your son and grant him the wisdom to understand the dangers of pride and stubbornness. Pray:

"Father, I pray that You open my son's eyes to see and understand the truth of Your Word. Give him a spirit of wisdom and revelation so that he may know You better and choose Your ways over the ways of the world."

Practical Steps to Reinforce Deliverance

While prayer is essential, practical steps are also necessary to reinforce the spiritual battle won in prayer. Here are a few strategies to consider:

- Encourage a Lifestyle of Humility: Model humility in your own life and encourage your son to serve others, demonstrating that greatness in the Kingdom of God comes through servanthood (Mark 10:43).

- Limit Exposure to Negative Influences: Be vigilant about the influences in your son's life that promote pride and rebellion. This may mean setting boundaries around media consumption, friendships, and activities that glorify self-centeredness or defiance against authority.

- Promote Godly Mentorship: Encourage relationships with mentors and leaders who exhibit humility and godliness. Sometimes, hearing truth from another trusted adult can make a significant impact.

- Consistent Affirmation and Love: Continually affirm your son's worth and value in Christ. Remind him that he is deeply loved, and his identity is secure in God, which can disarm the need to rely on pride or stubbornness as a defense mechanism.

- Teach and Discuss Biblical Truths: Create a habit of reading and discussing scriptures related to humility, obedience, and submission to God's will. The Word of God is a sword that cuts through lies and brings light to hidden areas of darkness.

Breaking the spirit of pride and stubbornness in your teenage son requires both spiritual and practical action. It is not a one-time event but a sustained effort in prayer, love, discipline, and truth. Trust that God is faithful to complete the work He has started (Philippians 1:6). Stand firm, equipped with the armor of God, and know that your prayers are powerful and effective in dismantling the strongholds of pride and rebellion in your son's life.

Praying for a Heart of Obedience and Submission to God

Obedience is the cornerstone of a vibrant and thriving relationship with God. It is the act of aligning our will with God's, surrendering our desires, and choosing His path over our own. For a teenage son navigating a world filled with temptations, peer pressures, and the growing desire for independence, cultivating a heart of obedience and submission to God can be a challenging, yet profoundly transformative process. As a parent, your prayers can become the catalyst for this transformation.

Understanding Rebellion: A Spiritual Perspective

Rebellion is more than mere disobedience; it is a spiritual condition rooted in pride, self-will, and the rejection of divine authority. The Bible reveals that rebellion is likened to the sin of witchcraft (1 Samuel 15:23). This stark comparison underscores the seriousness with which God views rebellion. It signifies a deliberate turning away from God's truth, embracing instead a mindset that resists His commands and standards. When a teenage son displays rebellious behavior, it is crucial to recognize that this is not just a developmental phase; it is a spiritual battle for his heart and soul.

The spirit of rebellion often manifests in subtle ways: refusal to listen to guidance, questioning authority, choosing friends or influences that lead away from God's truth, or even rejecting the values instilled by the family. Behind these behaviors, there can be spiritual forces at play that seek to separate your son from the love, protection, and guidance of the Heavenly Father. Recognizing this is the first step in effectively praying for a heart of obedience and submission to God.

The Biblical Foundation for Obedience

The Bible speaks extensively about the importance of obedience to God. In Deuteronomy 30:19-20, God sets before Israel a choice between life and death, blessing and curse, urging them to choose life by loving Him, obeying His voice, and holding fast to Him. This passage reveals that obedience is directly linked to life and blessing. It is not a set of restrictive rules but a pathway to divine favor and fulfillment.

Jesus Himself, the ultimate model of obedience, submitted to the will of the Father even unto death (Philippians 2:8). His obedience brought about the redemption of humanity, demonstrating that through obedience, God's purposes are fulfilled. When we pray for our teenage sons to have a heart of obedience, we are praying for them to align their lives with God's divine plan and experience the abundant life that Jesus promised in John 10:10.

Strategic Prayers for a Heart of Obedience

To effectively pray for a heart of obedience in your teenage son, consider focusing on these key areas:

1. Prayer for Revelation of God's Love

Rebellion often stems from a lack of understanding of God's love and character. Pray that your son would receive a revelation of God's unconditional love and grace. Ask the Holy Spirit to open his eyes to the depth of God's love, which compels us to trust and obey. Use scriptures like Ephesians 3:17-19 to guide your prayers: "…that Christ may dwell in your hearts through faith; that you, being rooted and grounded in love, may have strength to comprehend with all the saints what is the breadth and length and height and depth, and to know the love of Christ that surpasses knowledge, that you may be filled with all the fullness of God."

Pray that this revelation would dismantle every lie and misconception about God that fuels rebellion. As your son begins to grasp the love of God, his heart will naturally incline towards obedience, knowing that God's commands are not burdensome but are for his ultimate good (1 John 5:3).

2. Prayer for a Spirit of Humility
Rebellion is often fueled by pride — the desire to assert one's will above God's. Pray for the spirit of humility to be cultivated in your son's heart. Ask God to give him a teachable spirit, willing to receive instruction and correction. Use James 4:6 as a foundation: "God opposes the proud but gives grace to the humble."

Declare that your son will not be resistant to God's Word or the godly guidance of those placed in authority over him, such as parents, teachers, and spiritual leaders. Pray against the spirit of pride, and ask the Holy Spirit to soften his heart, making it responsive to God's truth.

3. Prayer for a Desire for God's Word

Pray that your son would develop a deep desire and hunger for God's Word. The Word of God is a light unto our path (Psalm 119:105) and provides the guidance needed for righteous living. Ask God to stir in him a passion for the scriptures, that he would find joy and delight in meditating on God's commands (Psalm 1:2).

As he immerses himself in the Word, he will learn to recognize God's voice and understand His will, which leads to obedience. Pray that every distraction and worldly allure that competes with his time and focus on God's Word be removed.

4. Prayer Against the Spirit of Rebellion

Boldly come against the spirit of rebellion in the name of Jesus. Recognize that rebellion is not just a personality trait but can be a spiritual stronghold that needs to be broken. Take authority in Jesus' name, declaring that rebellion has no place in your son's life. Pray for deliverance, binding the spirit of rebellion and loosing a spirit of obedience and submission to God (Matthew 18:18).

Use the authority given to you as a parent to command every rebellious thought, attitude, and action to bow to the name of Jesus. Declare that your son's mind, will, and emotions are aligned with the will of God.

5. Prayer for Godly Influences and Role Models

Pray that God would place godly mentors and role models in your son's life who will exemplify a life of obedience and submission to God. Ask the Lord to surround him with friends who encourage righteousness and uphold godly values (Proverbs 13:20).

Pray for divine connections, that he may encounter individuals who will speak truth into his life, guide him in love, and model a lifestyle of faithfulness and obedience to God. Ask God to remove any negative influences that may lead him astray and replace them with people who will positively impact his spiritual journey.

Walking in Victory Over Rebellion

As you pray with specificity, fervency, and faith, believe that God is at work in your son's heart, transforming it day by day. Prayer is a powerful weapon that can break every chain of rebellion and disobedience, replacing it with a heart fully submitted to the loving authority of God. Remember that while the process may take time, persistence in prayer, coupled with unwavering faith in God's promises, will yield the fruit of righteousness and obedience in your son's life. Trust God to complete the good work He has begun in your son, believing that his heart will turn wholly toward the Lord, reflecting His love and grace to the world around him.

Rebuking the Spirit of Disobedience and Defiance

The spirit of disobedience and defiance can often manifest subtly, growing like a weed in the garden of a young person's heart. This spirit, characterized by a refusal to submit to God's authority or the guidance of loving parents, can lead a teenager down a dangerous path filled with rebellion, anger, and estrangement from the very source of life—God Himself.

The Spiritual Roots of Rebellion

Rebellion is not merely a behavioral issue; it is deeply spiritual, rooted in the sin nature that every human being inherits from Adam. The Bible teaches us that rebellion is akin to witchcraft (1 Samuel 15:23), which reveals the seriousness of defiance against God's will. The enemy seeks to exploit this rebellious nature, especially during the tumultuous teenage years, when identity and independence are being formed. The spirit of disobedience thrives in an atmosphere where God's Word is disregarded, where respect for authority is dismissed, and where pride reigns unchecked.

We must recognize that this battle is not against flesh and blood, but against spiritual forces of evil (Ephesians 6:12). Therefore, our approach to rebuking the spirit of disobedience and defiance must be firmly rooted in spiritual warfare, utilizing the weapons God has given us: the Word of God, the name of Jesus, and the power of prayer.

Rebuking the Spirit: Standing in Your Authority

As a parent, you have a unique spiritual authority over your home and family. God has entrusted you with the spiritual nurturing and protection of your children. To rebuke the spirit of disobedience, you must first recognize your authority in Christ. Jesus declared in Luke 10:19, "I have given you authority to trample on snakes and scorpions and to overcome all the power of the enemy; nothing will harm you." This authority is not passive—it requires action.

Begin by setting aside time for prayer and fasting, seeking God's guidance and wisdom on how to approach this specific battle. Ask the Holy Spirit to reveal any hidden areas of disobedience or rebellion that need to be addressed. Be prepared to confront not only the spiritual forces at work but also any patterns of behavior or communication in your home that may be contributing to the problem.

When you pray, speak directly to the spirit of disobedience. Declare that it has no place in your son's life or in your home. Use scriptures as your weapon: "Submit yourselves, then, to God. Resist the devil, and he will flee from you" (James 4:7). Proclaim that your son is under the lordship of Jesus Christ, and that every spirit of rebellion, defiance, and disobedience must bow to the name of Jesus. Remember that you are not battling in your own strength but in the strength of the Lord.

The Role of Confession and Repentance

Rebuking the spirit of disobedience is not just about casting out a spiritual force; it's also about cultivating a heart of repentance in your son. Encourage your teenage son to engage in self-examination. Create a safe space where he feels comfortable discussing his struggles, doubts, and frustrations. Help him to understand that rebellion separates us from God's love and blessings. Guide him to confess his sins, not out of fear or guilt, but out of a desire to be right with God.

Lead your son in prayers of repentance, using Psalm 51 as a guide. David's cry for mercy, cleansing, and renewal is a powerful model of what genuine repentance looks like. Encourage your son to pray, "Create in me a pure heart, O God, and renew a steadfast spirit within me" (Psalm 51:10). Help him understand that repentance is a daily choice, a turning away from sin, and a turning toward God. As your son begins to embrace repentance, you will see a breaking down of the walls of rebellion and a softening of his heart toward God.

Replacing Rebellion with Righteousness

Deliverance is not complete until what has been removed is replaced with God's righteousness and truth. Jesus teaches in Matthew 12:43-45 that when an evil spirit leaves a person, it seeks to return to find the house "empty, swept, and put in order." If the house is not filled with the presence of God, that spirit will come back with even more evil companions. Therefore, it is crucial to fill your son's heart and mind with God's Word and righteous desires.

Encourage him to read and meditate on the Bible daily. Help him to memorize key scriptures that speak against rebellion and defiance, such as Proverbs 3:5-6, "Trust in the Lord with all your heart and lean not on your own understanding; in all your ways submit to him, and he will make your paths straight." Encourage him to cultivate a habit of worship, which invites God's presence and dispels the darkness. Surround him with godly mentors and friends who can provide support, accountability, and encouragement in his spiritual walk.

Maintaining Vigilance: A Lifelong Commitment

The journey to deliverance from a spirit of rebellion is not a one-time event but a continuous process. Stay vigilant in prayer, continually covering your son with prayers of protection, wisdom, and guidance. Speak life and truth into his life regularly, reminding him of his identity in Christ. Encourage him to stay connected to the local church and engage in activities that promote spiritual growth.

Be prepared for setbacks, and do not lose heart when they occur. Remember that God's timing is perfect and that every prayer you pray is a seed planted in faith. Hold on to the promise of Galatians 6:9, "Let us not become weary in doing good, for at the proper time we will reap a harvest if we do not give up."

Rebuking the spirit of disobedience and defiance requires a firm stance in spiritual authority, a commitment to prayer and fasting, a focus on repentance and confession, and an ongoing effort to replace rebellion with righteousness. It is a battle fought on your knees, but it is a battle you do not fight alone—God is with you, empowering you every step of the way to see your son walk in freedom, victory, and obedience to Christ.

Restoring Respect for Authority and Godly Leadership

Restoring Respect for Authority and Godly Leadership is an essential aspect of spiritual deliverance for a teenage son struggling with rebellion and disobedience. The spirit of rebellion is not merely a teenage phase; it is a spiritual battle that has its roots in the heart and manifests through behavior, attitude, and choices.

The Root of Rebellion: A Spiritual Perspective

Rebellion, according to the Bible, is like the sin of witchcraft (1 Samuel 15:23). This means it is not just a behavioral issue but a deep-seated spiritual condition that opposes God's order. From a Christian perspective, rebellion begins when an individual, especially a young person, begins to reject the rightful authority of parents, teachers, and ultimately, God. This rejection often stems from a wounded heart, unmet emotional needs, or a desire for control and independence.

As parents, it's crucial to recognize that the battle against rebellion is not fought merely with human wisdom or punishment but with spiritual weapons. Ephesians 6:12 reminds us that "we wrestle not against flesh and blood, but against principalities, against powers, against the rulers of the darkness of this world, against spiritual wickedness in high places." Therefore, the first step in restoring respect for authority is recognizing the spiritual nature of rebellion and addressing it through prayer and biblical instruction.

Prayers for Breaking the Spirit of Rebellion

To restore respect for authority, parents must begin by interceding fervently and specifically against the spirit of rebellion. Here are a few targeted prayers to consider:

- Prayer of Repentance: Begin by repenting on behalf of your family line for any generational patterns of rebellion against authority. Confess any known instances where you or your ancestors may have dishonored authority, asking God to break any curses associated with disobedience (Exodus 20:5-6).

- Prayer for a Heart of Obedience: Ask God to replace your son's heart of stone with a heart of flesh that is open and responsive to Him (Ezekiel 36:26). Pray that your son will develop a genuine desire to honor God and those in authority over him.

- Prayer Against the Spirit of Pride: The spirit of rebellion is often linked with pride. Pray against the spirit of pride that seeks to elevate your son's will above God's will. Declare humility over his life, asking God to humble him under His mighty hand (James 4:10).

- Prayer for Spiritual Armor: Daily, put on the full armor of God on behalf of your son (Ephesians 6:13-17). Specifically, declare the helmet of salvation to guard his mind against thoughts of rebellion, the breastplate of righteousness to protect his heart, and the sword of the Spirit—the Word of God—to cut down any rebellious thoughts or attitudes.

- Declaration of Authority: Speak life and authority into your son's identity. Declare that he is created to be a leader under God's authority, that he has the mind of Christ (1 Corinthians 2:16), and that he will walk in obedience, honor, and submission to God's order.

Teaching Biblical Respect for Authority

In addition to prayer, it is essential to teach your son what the Bible says about authority and respect. This teaching is more than just quoting scriptures; it involves modeling, explaining, and discussing biblical principles in a way that connects with his daily experiences and struggles.

- The Biblical Basis for Authority: Start by explaining that all authority comes from God. Romans 13:1 states, "Let every soul be subject to the governing authorities, for there is no authority except from God, and the authorities that exist are appointed by God." Help your son understand that respecting authority is ultimately an act of obedience to God.

- Christ as the Ultimate Example: Point to Jesus Christ, who demonstrated perfect submission to the Father, even unto death (Philippians 2:8). Help your son see that Jesus, though He had every right to assert His authority, chose to submit Himself to God's plan. Encourage him to follow Christ's example, recognizing that true strength lies in humility and obedience.

- Consequences of Rebellion: Use biblical stories like that of Korah's rebellion (Numbers 16) and the fall of King Saul (1 Samuel 15) to illustrate the dangers of rejecting God-given authority. Discuss how these stories show that rebellion leads to destruction, while obedience brings blessings.

- The Blessings of Honor: Reinforce the promise of Ephesians 6:2-3: "Honor your father and mother"—which is the first commandment with a promise—"so that it may go well with you and that you may enjoy long life on the earth." Explain that honoring authority is not just a duty but a path to divine favor and long life.

Practical Steps for Restoring Respect

Beyond prayer and biblical teaching, there are practical steps parents can take to help their son restore respect for authority:

- Modeling Respectful Behavior: As a parent, it is crucial to model the respect for authority that you wish to see in your son. Speak respectfully about teachers, pastors, government leaders, and others in positions of authority. Your son will learn more from what you do than from what you say.

- Creating Opportunities for Responsibility: Encourage your son to take on responsibilities at home, school, or church. Give him opportunities to make decisions and experience the consequences of his actions in a controlled environment. This helps him understand the value of submitting to authority and the impact of his choices.

- Establishing Clear Boundaries: Be clear about your expectations for behavior and the consequences of disobedience. Consistency is key; when your son knows there are consequences for disrespecting authority, he is more likely to understand the importance of honor.

- Open Dialogue and Understanding: Create a safe space for your son to express his feelings about authority. Sometimes, rebellion stems from frustration or misunderstanding. Listen actively and empathetically, and address any concerns or misconceptions he may have about those in authority.

- Positive Reinforcement: Celebrate moments when your son demonstrates respect for authority, no matter how small. Acknowledge his efforts and reinforce that he is on the right path. Positive reinforcement can build confidence and encourage continued growth in this area.

Standing Firm in Faith and Perseverance

Restoring respect for authority in your teenage son is not a quick fix but a spiritual journey that requires perseverance, patience, and unwavering faith. Remember that God is on your side in this battle, and His Word is a powerful weapon against any spirit of rebellion. Keep praying, keep teaching, and keep trusting that in His time, God will bring a full transformation to your son's heart and life.

In this journey, you are not alone. The Lord promises in Isaiah 54:13, "All your children will be taught by the Lord, and great will be their peace." Stand on this promise, and know that as you continue to pray and guide your son, God will work in his heart, bringing him to a place of honor, respect, and godly submission to authority.

Encouraging Humility and a Teachable Spirit

Humility and a teachable spirit are essential virtues in the Christian journey, especially for a teenager navigating the complexities of growing up in today's world. A heart that is humble before God is open to His correction, guidance, and transformation. As a parent, your role in fostering these virtues in your teenage son is crucial.

The Biblical Foundation of Humility

Humility is foundational to Christian character. In James 4:6, the Bible says, "God opposes the proud but shows favor to the humble." This verse underscores the importance of humility, not just as a virtue, but as a requirement for divine favor and grace. Jesus Himself, the ultimate example of humility, demonstrated this through His life and teachings. Philippians 2:5-8 describes how He, being in the very nature of God, did not consider equality with God something to be used to His advantage. Instead, He emptied Himself, taking on the form of a servant, and became obedient to death on a cross.

Encouraging your son to embrace humility means guiding him to understand that it is not a sign of weakness, but a strength. Humility allows him to recognize his need for God, depend on God's grace, and be open to learning from others. It is a quality that sets the foundation for a teachable spirit—a willingness to learn, to be corrected, and to grow.

Praying for Humility and a Teachable Spirit

Prayer is the first and most powerful tool in encouraging humility and a teachable spirit. Begin by lifting up your son to God in prayer, asking that God will soften his heart and open his mind to receive His truth. Pray specifically for the breaking down of pride, arrogance, and any spirit of stubbornness that may hinder his spiritual growth.

An example of a powerful prayer could be:

"Father, I lift my son to you today. I ask that you give him a heart like David's—humble, repentant, and teachable. Break down any walls of pride and arrogance. Remove the spirit of stubbornness and rebellion that resists your truth. Open his heart to receive your wisdom and guidance. May he seek to learn and grow in your ways. Grant him a spirit of humility, that he may always be willing to listen, to be corrected, and to follow your path. In Jesus' name, Amen."

Prayers such as this, grounded in faith and expectation, invite the Holy Spirit to work in your son's life. They create a spiritual atmosphere that is conducive to change and transformation.

Creating a Culture of Humility at Home

Humility and a teachable spirit are best taught through example. Your home should be a place where humility is celebrated and practiced. As a parent, be intentional in modeling humility in your daily interactions. Admit when you are wrong, ask for forgiveness, and show respect to others, including your son. This teaches him that humility is not about belittling oneself, but about acknowledging one's limitations and valuing others.

Encourage open and honest communication, where your son feels safe to express his thoughts and feelings without fear of harsh judgment. When he makes mistakes, use these moments as teaching opportunities rather than occasions for harsh criticism. Emphasize that everyone makes mistakes, and what is important is the willingness to learn from them.

Using Scripture to Shape a Humble Heart

The Word of God is a powerful tool in shaping character. Encourage your son to meditate on scriptures that highlight the importance of humility. Verses such as Proverbs 3:5-6, "Trust in the Lord with all your heart and lean not on your own understanding," and Micah 6:8, "He has shown you, O mortal, what is good. And what does the Lord require of you? To act justly and to love mercy and to walk humbly with your God," can serve as daily reminders of the value God places on humility.

Encourage your son to write these verses down, memorize them, and pray them back to God. You could also initiate a Bible study together, focusing on the lives of biblical characters who displayed humility, such as Moses, David, and, above all, Jesus Christ. Discuss how these individuals were used mightily by God because of their humble hearts.

Reinforcing Humility through Service

One of the most effective ways to foster humility is through service to others. Encourage your son to engage in acts of service, whether within the family, church, or community. Volunteering at a local charity, helping with church activities, or even assisting an elderly neighbor can teach him the value of putting others before himself.

Service provides a tangible way to practice humility. It shifts the focus from self-centered desires to meeting the needs of others. Through service, your son can experience firsthand the joy that comes from giving and the fulfillment that comes from living according to God's commands.

Addressing Pride and Encouraging Teachability

A teachable spirit cannot coexist with pride. Pride blinds individuals to their faults and creates resistance to correction. Help your son recognize the dangers of pride and its destructive effects. Share biblical stories, such as King Saul's downfall, which resulted from pride and disobedience, contrasting them with stories of those who embraced correction, like King

David, who repented and sought God's mercy when confronted with his sin.

Encourage your son to seek wisdom from others—mentors, teachers, and spiritual leaders. Cultivate an environment where questioning and learning are celebrated, not discouraged. Reinforce the idea that being teachable is a sign of strength and wisdom, not weakness. Remind him of Proverbs 12:1, which states, "Whoever loves discipline loves knowledge, but whoever hates correction is stupid."

Bold Steps for Fostering a Teachable Spirit

Encouraging humility and a teachable spirit is not just about avoiding pride; it's about actively pursuing growth. Challenge your son to set goals for personal and spiritual growth. This could include reading Christian literature, attending Bible study groups, or participating in church activities that require collaboration and learning from others.

A bold step in this journey is helping your son find a mentor—a trusted Christian leader who can provide guidance, accountability, and encouragement. A mentor can offer a different perspective, share wisdom from personal experience, and help your son navigate life's challenges with a humble and open heart.

Fostering humility and a teachable spirit in your teenage son requires a combination of prayer, example, scripture, service, and intentional teaching. It is a journey that requires patience, persistence, and faith, trusting that God, who began a good work in your son, will carry it on to completion (Philippians 1:6). Encourage your son to remain humble before God and open to His guidance, knowing that in doing so, he aligns himself with God's perfect will and favor for his life.

Deliverance Prayers

1. Heavenly Father, in the name of Jesus, I take authority over every spirit of pride and stubbornness that seeks to control my son's heart and mind. I declare that he will walk in humility and submission to your will, breaking free from the chains of arrogance. Amen.

2. Lord Jesus, I bind and rebuke the spirit of rebellion that tries to lead my son away from your truth. In your mighty name, I speak obedience and a surrendered heart over him. I declare that every influence of defiance is broken right now. Amen.

3. Father, in Jesus' name, I ask for a fresh anointing over my son's life, softening his heart to hear and obey your voice. Remove any hardness of heart or resistance to your Word. I command every spirit of disobedience to leave him now, in Jesus' name. Amen.

4. Lord, I pray for my son to have a teachable spirit, willing to learn from you and others you place in his life. I come against every prideful thought

that exalts itself against the knowledge of God, and I declare that he will grow in wisdom and understanding. Amen.

5. In the name of Jesus, I break every curse of rebellion over my son's life, both generational and personal. I declare that he is set free by the blood of Jesus and will walk in submission and respect for authority according to God's design. Amen.

6. Father, in Jesus' name, I command every spirit of pride that blinds my son's eyes from seeing his need for you to be removed. I pray that he will see himself as you see him and be drawn into a deeper relationship with you. Amen.

7. Lord Jesus, I rebuke the spirit of stubbornness that prevents my son from receiving godly counsel and instruction. I declare that his ears are open to your voice and that he will follow your guidance with a humble heart. Amen.

8. In Jesus' name, I take authority over every stronghold of rebellion in my son's life. I declare that these strongholds are torn down by the power of the Holy Spirit and replaced with a spirit of obedience and love for your commandments. Amen.

9. Heavenly Father, I pray that my son will be filled with a deep sense of your love that overpowers any rebellious tendencies. In Jesus' name, I

command every spirit that opposes your love to flee. May he find joy and peace in walking in your ways. Amen.

10. Lord, I declare that my son is no longer a slave to the spirit of disobedience. In Jesus' name, I pray that he will have a renewed desire to honor you with his actions, words, and thoughts, choosing your path over any rebellious way. Amen.

11. Father, I speak life and truth over my son in Jesus' name. I declare that every lie the enemy has spoken to him about rebelling against authority is silenced. May he know the joy and freedom of living a life that pleases you. Amen.

12. In the powerful name of Jesus, I break every agreement my son has made, knowingly or unknowingly, with the spirit of pride. I declare that he will walk in humility, knowing that true greatness comes from serving you and others. Amen.

13. Lord, I bind the spirit of stubbornness that seeks to close my son's heart to your correction. In Jesus' name, I declare that he will receive your discipline as a sign of your love and will grow in righteousness and holiness. Amen.

14. In the name of Jesus, I take authority over every rebellious attitude and thought pattern in my son's life. I declare that he will have the mind of Christ, valuing obedience, humility, and submission to your will. Amen.

15. Father, I pray for a heart of flesh for my son, soft and receptive to your Word. In Jesus' name, I bind every spirit of defiance and declare that he will walk in a spirit of meekness, esteeming others higher than himself. Amen.

16. Lord Jesus, I command the spirit of disobedience to leave my son's life now. I declare that he is covered by your grace and truth, and that he will walk in righteousness, choosing your ways over his own desires. Amen.

17. In Jesus' name, I rebuke every demonic influence that tries to provoke my son into rebellious behavior. I declare that he will be filled with the Holy Spirit, led by your guidance, and protected from any ungodly temptations. Amen.

18. Father, in the name of Jesus, I come against every spirit of rebellion that seeks to separate my son from your love. I declare that he will experience your unconditional love and will desire to honor you in all he does. Amen.

19. Lord, I take authority in Jesus' name over any spirit of pride that prevents my son from admitting his mistakes. I pray for a spirit of humility and repentance, that he may turn to you with a contrite heart and find forgiveness and restoration. Amen.

20. In the name of Jesus, I declare that my son will break free from any rebellious friends or influences that draw him away from your path. I pray that you will surround him with godly friendships that encourage obedience and faith. Amen.

21. Father, in Jesus' name, I pray for a renewed mind for my son, that he may reject every thought of rebellion and embrace your truth. I declare that his mind will be filled with your Word, leading him to a life of obedience and submission to you. Amen.

22. Lord Jesus, I speak against the spirit of defiance that challenges every authority in my son's life. I declare that he will respect and honor those in leadership, seeing them as appointed by you, and will walk in peace and submission. Amen.

23. In Jesus' name, I declare that my son is released from the grip of rebellion. I pray for an outpouring of your grace upon him, enabling him to choose your ways over his own, bringing glory to your name in every decision. Amen.

24. Father, I command every spirit of pride and rebellion to bow to the authority of Jesus Christ. I declare that my son is free, that he will experience the joy of obedience, and that he will live a life that reflects your glory. Amen.

25. Lord, in the mighty name of Jesus, I pray that my son's heart will be aligned with your heart. I declare that he will walk in obedience, humility, and love, shining as a light for your Kingdom, free from every spirit of rebellion. Amen.

Chapter 7

Declaring Victory: Sustaining Your Son's Deliverance

Creating a Daily Prayer Strategy for Continued Freedom

As a parent standing in the gap for your teenage son, creating a daily prayer strategy is not just a routine—it's an act of warfare, a declaration of faith, and a spiritual covering that sustains the freedom God has given. Deliverance is not a one-time event; it is a process that requires vigilance, consistency, and faith. The enemy is relentless, and as such, our prayer life must be even more relentless. To ensure your son remains in the freedom Christ has purchased, this section focuses on creating a daily prayer strategy that is both comprehensive and effective.

1. Begin with Praise and Worship: Invoking God's Presence

The foundation of a powerful daily prayer strategy is to begin with praise and worship. Psalm 22:3 tells us that God inhabits the praises of His people. When we worship, we invite God's presence into our midst. Begin each day by thanking God for His goodness and declaring His majesty. Praise Him for who He is and for what He has done in your son's life. This act not only sets the spiritual atmosphere but also shifts your focus from the problem to the One who has the power to deliver.

Start your morning prayer by singing a hymn or listening to a worship song that speaks to God's power and faithfulness. Declare God's greatness over your son's life. Say, "Father, you are mighty and powerful. You are the deliverer, the One who breaks every chain. I exalt your name today, and I thank you for the freedom you have given to my son." This simple act of praise will awaken your spirit and align your heart with God's purposes.

2. Declare the Word of God: The Sword of the Spirit

Hebrews 4:12 describes God's Word as living, active, and sharper than any double-edged sword. To create a strong daily prayer strategy, incorporate specific Scriptures that address your son's areas of struggle and the promises of God regarding his freedom. The Word of God is not just words on a page; it is a weapon of warfare, a powerful declaration that pierces through darkness and establishes God's truth in your son's life.

Find passages that speak directly to the issues your son is facing. For instance, if your son struggles with fear, declare 2 Timothy 1:7: "For God has not given us a spirit of fear, but of power and of love and of a sound mind." If he battles temptation, use 1 Corinthians 10:13: "No temptation has overtaken you except what is common to mankind. And God is faithful; he will not let you be tempted beyond what you can bear."

Speak these Scriptures out loud over your son every day. Declare them with authority, believing that the Word of God is alive and active. You could say, "In the name of Jesus, I declare that my son has not been given a spirit of fear but of power, love, and a sound mind. He is strong in the Lord and in the power of His might. He will not fall into temptation, for the Lord provides a way of escape." This active use of Scripture builds a spiritual shield around your son, protecting him from attacks and reinforcing his deliverance.

3. Engage in Intercessory Prayer: Standing in the Gap

Intercessory prayer is standing in the gap on behalf of another. Ezekiel 22:30 tells us that God is searching for someone to stand in the gap for others. As a parent, you are called to be that intercessor for your son. Each day, dedicate time to pray fervently for his protection, spiritual growth, and continued freedom. Pray specifically, pray boldly, and pray with expectation.

Begin by praying for God's hedge of protection around your son, as in Job 1:10, where Satan himself acknowledges the protective hedge God placed around Job. Ask God to send His angels to guard your son in all his ways (Psalm 91:11). Pray for your son's heart to be softened and open to the Holy Spirit's guidance and conviction. Declare that any plans the enemy has for your son will be thwarted in Jesus' name.

"Father, in the name of Jesus, I stand in the gap for my son today. I declare that he is surrounded by your divine protection, that no weapon formed against him will prosper, and every tongue that rises against him in judgment, you will condemn (Isaiah 54:17). I ask that you open his heart to your voice, that he would be sensitive to your leading, and that he would walk in the freedom you have already given him."

4. Establish a Prayer Routine: Morning, Noon, and Night

Daniel prayed three times a day, a habit that sustained him through great trials (Daniel 6:10). Consistency is key in spiritual warfare. Set specific times throughout the day for prayer. This does not mean you have to spend hours in prayer each time, but rather, that you maintain a constant communication line with God. Morning prayers can focus on covering your son with protection and strength for the day ahead. Midday prayers can be brief but powerful declarations of God's promises, and evening prayers can focus on thanksgiving and reflection on what God has done.

Create a practical schedule that aligns with your daily routine. Perhaps you pray in the morning before your son wakes up, a quick prayer during lunch, and a more extended time in the evening after dinner. The goal is to create a rhythm that keeps your son covered in prayer throughout the day.

5. Engage Your Son in Prayer: Teaching Him to Fight His Battles

While you are praying for your son, it is equally important to teach him how to pray for himself. Equip him with the knowledge and tools he needs to fight his own battles. Encourage him to pray daily, even if it is just for a few minutes. Share Scriptures with him that he can declare over his own life. Model prayer for him, and invite him to join you in family prayer times.

Discuss with him the importance of personal prayer and how it empowers him to resist temptation and draw closer to God. Encourage him to be honest with God about his struggles, to confess his sins, and to ask for help in moments of weakness. Let him see that prayer is not just a religious duty but a lifeline, a source of strength, and a direct line of communication with his Creator.

"Son, I want you to know that prayer is powerful. It is not just something we do because we are Christians; it is our weapon, our strength, and our shield. Whenever you feel afraid, tempted, or lost, call on the name of Jesus. Speak the Word of God over your life. You have the authority to command any evil influence to leave in Jesus' name. Remember, you are never alone—God is with you, and He hears you every time you pray."

Sustaining Freedom Through Prayer

A daily prayer strategy is essential for sustaining your son's deliverance and freedom. This is not a passive endeavor but an active, ongoing spiritual battle that requires dedication and faith. By beginning with praise, declaring the Word, engaging in intercessory prayer, establishing a prayer routine, and teaching your son to pray, you create a spiritual shield that surrounds him daily. Remember, you are not fighting for victory; you are fighting from a place of victory because Christ has already won. Stay committed, stay fervent, and trust that God is faithful to complete the work He has begun in your son's life (Philippians 1:6).

Building a Wall of Prayer Around Your Home and Family

In the battle for the spiritual well-being of your teenage son, prayer is not just a tool; it is your greatest weapon, your strongest shield, and your most strategic defense. Here, we focus on the concept of "Building a Wall of Prayer," an ancient biblical principle that is as relevant today as it was in the times of Nehemiah, who led the Israelites in rebuilding the walls of Jerusalem. Just as physical walls protect a city from external enemies, a spiritual wall of prayer around your home and family creates a powerful barrier against the onslaughts of the enemy, securing divine protection and fostering an atmosphere of peace and godliness.

Understanding the Need for a Wall of Prayer

The Bible speaks extensively about the importance of protection and defense. In Nehemiah 4:9, we see a clear example: "But we prayed to our God and posted a guard day and night to meet this threat." Nehemiah understood that rebuilding the walls of Jerusalem was not only a physical endeavor but a spiritual one, requiring constant vigilance and prayer. Today, as a parent standing in the gap for your teenage son, you must also be vigilant, building a spiritual fortress that guards against the enemy's attempts to infiltrate your home and affect your family dynamics.

A "wall of prayer" is a spiritual barricade composed of daily, intentional, and faith-filled prayers. It is not built overnight but is a continuous, deliberate act of spiritual warfare, fueled by a deep understanding of God's promises and a firm belief in His power to protect and deliver. This wall is constructed brick by brick—each brick representing a prayer of faith, a declaration of God's Word, and a plea for divine intervention. Your goal is to create an environment where God's presence is palpably felt, and His protection is ever-present.

Practical Steps to Building Your Wall of Prayer

1. Establish a Daily Prayer Routine: Your Foundation

Just as a wall requires a solid foundation, your spiritual barrier must begin with a consistent, daily prayer routine. This involves setting aside dedicated time each day to pray fervently for your son, your home, and your entire family. Start by choosing a specific time that works best for you—whether early in the morning, during a quiet afternoon break, or late at night. Consistency is key. Remember, the strength of a wall lies in the uniformity and reliability of its construction. As you pray daily, your prayers lay a steady foundation that grows stronger with time.

2. Incorporate Scripture into Your Prayers: Your Building Blocks

God's Word is your primary material for building this wall. Hebrews 4:12 reminds us that "the word of God is alive and active, sharper than any double-edged sword." When you pray scripture over your home, you are not merely uttering words; you are wielding a mighty weapon that can penetrate the darkest situations. Select specific verses that address protection, deliverance, and God's promises for your family. Verses like Psalm 91, Ephesians 6:10-18, and Isaiah 54:17 serve as building blocks that fortify your wall, creating an impenetrable defense against spiritual attacks.

3. Anoint Your Home: Your Sacred Boundary Markers

In the Old Testament, anointing with oil was a sign of sanctification, setting apart people or places for God's holy purposes. Consider physically anointing your home with oil, a symbolic act that marks your home as a place of God's presence and authority. Walk through each room, praying and anointing doorposts and windows, declaring that every space within your home belongs to the Lord and is under His protection. This act can be a powerful spiritual statement, a bold proclamation that your home is a sanctuary against the enemy's influence.

4. Engage in Spiritual Warfare Prayers: Your Defensive Arsenal

As you pray, incorporate prayers of spiritual warfare, taking authority over any strongholds or negative spiritual influences trying to gain a foothold in your home or in your son's life. Use the authority given to you in Luke 10:19: "I have given you authority to trample on snakes and scorpions and to overcome all the power of the enemy; nothing will harm you." Command any spirit of rebellion, fear, depression, or any other negative force to leave in Jesus' name. Declare aloud that no weapon formed against your family shall prosper (Isaiah 54:17). These prayers act as defensive weapons that reinforce your wall, pushing back against any enemy encroachment.

5. Create a Prayer Chain: Your Community Support System

No wall stands firm without the reinforcement of interconnected support. Invite other believers to join you in prayer for your son and your family. This could be a small group of trusted friends, your church prayer group, or even an online community of prayer warriors. Establish a prayer chain where each person commits to pray at a specific time or day. As Matthew 18:20 reminds us, "For where two or three gather in my name, there am I with them." The combined strength of communal prayer reinforces the spiritual wall around your family, ensuring it stands firm against the enemy's attacks.

Expanding the Wall: Praying for Every Aspect of Your Son's Life

To ensure your wall of prayer is complete, extend your prayers to cover every aspect of your son's life. Pray for his relationships—friends, teachers, mentors, and future spouse—that they will be godly influences, guiding him in the ways of the Lord. Pray for his mental and emotional health, asking God to fill him with peace, joy, and wisdom. Pray for his academic pursuits and future career, that he may discover his God-given purpose and walk in his calling. Cover every detail with prayer, leaving no area unprotected.

Maintaining the Wall: A Continuous Effort

A wall of prayer, once built, requires maintenance. The enemy is relentless, and so must you be in your spiritual vigilance. Keep your prayer life fresh and dynamic; do not let it become a monotonous routine. Regularly assess the spiritual condition of your home and family, seeking the Holy Spirit's guidance on how to pray specifically and strategically. Keep adding bricks to your wall—new prayers, new scriptures, new declarations of faith—ensuring that it remains strong and unbreakable.

The Outcome: Living Within God's Fortress

When you build and maintain this wall of prayer, you create a fortress—a sanctuary where God's presence is the reigning force. Your home becomes a place where peace, righteousness, and godly character thrive, and your son finds refuge from the world's pressures and temptations. You will begin to see transformation—not just in your son's life, but throughout your family. By establishing this wall, you are declaring that your home belongs to the Lord, and you are trusting in His divine protection, guidance, and grace to sustain you through every challenge.

Remember, this wall is not just a defensive structure but a powerful testimony of faith. It is a living, breathing testament to the victory that is already yours in Christ. Keep praying, keep believing, and watch as God honors your commitment, fortifying your home and family against every spiritual threat.

Equipping Your Son with Spiritual Weapons for Battle

In the spiritual battle for your teenage son's deliverance and freedom, one of the most critical strategies is equipping him with the spiritual weapons necessary to stand firm against the forces of darkness. As a parent, your role isn't just to pray for him but to actively teach and empower him to use the tools God has provided to resist the enemy and walk in victory.

Understanding the Nature of the Battle

The Bible clearly states that our battle is not against flesh and blood but against spiritual forces of evil in the heavenly realms (Ephesians 6:12). For many parents, the spiritual struggles of their teenage sons may appear to be behavioral problems, attitude issues, or mere teenage rebellion. However, behind these manifestations often lies a spiritual battle that requires a spiritual response.

The enemy's tactics are not new; they are designed to deceive, intimidate, and destroy. Teenagers are particularly vulnerable due to their developmental stage, where they are discovering their identities and facing immense peer pressure, societal expectations, and emotional challenges.

This is why it is crucial to help your son understand that his struggles are not just psychological or emotional but are deeply spiritual. He needs to see himself as a soldier in God's army, equipped and ready to fight for his freedom and destiny.

The Armor of God: A Practical Application for Your Son

The Apostle Paul provides a blueprint for spiritual warfare in Ephesians 6:10-18, where he outlines the Armor of God. Each piece of this armor represents a critical weapon that your son must learn to wield effectively:

- The Belt of Truth: Help your son to fasten the belt of truth around his life. Truth is the foundation upon which all other spiritual weapons rest. Encourage him to read the Bible daily, meditate on its truths, and memorize key verses. When he is armed with the truth, he will be able to discern the lies of the enemy that come through various channels—whether they be social media, peers, or even his own internal doubts and fears. Challenge him to speak the truth boldly, to reject falsehood, and to stand for what is right, even when it is unpopular.

- The Breastplate of Righteousness: The breastplate protects the heart, which is the wellspring of life (Proverbs 4:23). Teach your son that righteousness is not about being perfect but about having a right relationship with God through Jesus Christ. He needs to understand the importance of repentance and the power of the blood of Jesus to cleanse him from all unrighteousness (1 John 1:9). Encourage him to live a life of integrity, making decisions that honor God and reflect His righteousness. Explain that every act of obedience strengthens his breastplate, making him less vulnerable to the enemy's attacks.

- The Shoes of the Gospel of Peace: Equip your son with a solid understanding of the Gospel of Jesus Christ. He should be ready to share his faith and live in a way that reflects the peace of God, which surpasses all understanding (Philippians 4:7). Teach him that peace is both a defense and an offense. When his heart is anchored in God's peace, he will not be easily shaken by the chaos around him. Encourage him to be a peacemaker in his school, social circles, and family, spreading the message of God's love and reconciliation.

- The Shield of Faith: Faith is a powerful defense against the fiery darts of the enemy. Help your son to develop a strong, unwavering faith by sharing testimonies of God's faithfulness, both in the Bible and in your family's history. Encourage him to write down his own testimonies—moments where he has seen God move in his life. These testimonies become a personal shield that deflects the enemy's lies. Explain that faith is not passive; it is active trust in God's promises, even when circumstances seem contrary.

- The Helmet of Salvation: The mind is a primary battlefield in spiritual warfare. Teach your son to guard his thoughts and to wear the helmet of salvation with confidence. Remind him that his identity is rooted in Christ and that he is saved by grace through faith (Ephesians 2:8-9).

Encourage him to take every thought captive and make it obedient to Christ (2 Corinthians 10:5). Teach him practical ways to renew his mind, such as meditating on God's Word, rejecting negative thoughts, and replacing them with God's promises.

- The Sword of the Spirit, Which Is the Word of God: This is the only offensive weapon in the Armor of God, and it represents the spoken Word of God. Teach your son to wield the Word of God as a sword against the enemy's attacks. Encourage him to memorize scriptures and use them in prayer. Explain how Jesus defeated Satan in the wilderness by saying, "It is written..." (Matthew 4:1-11). Teach your son to do the same—when he is tempted, discouraged, or under spiritual attack, he can speak God's Word boldly and declare victory.

- Praying in the Spirit on All Occasions: Prayer is the battlefield where victory is won. Teach your son that prayer is more than a ritual; it is a powerful weapon. Encourage him to pray without ceasing (1 Thessalonians 5:17), to pray in the Spirit, and to intercede for himself and others. Help him understand the importance of praying with authority, using the name of Jesus to break strongholds, bind the enemy, and declare God's will over his life.

Practical Steps to Equip Your Son

- Daily Devotions Together: Set aside time each day to read the Bible and pray with your son. Teach him how to use scriptures in prayer and to declare them over his life.

- Encourage Spiritual Disciplines: Encourage him to fast, meditate, and practice other spiritual disciplines that strengthen his walk with God. Help him understand the power of these practices in breaking strongholds.

- Model Spiritual Warfare: Lead by example. Let your son see you praying, interceding, and standing firm in faith. Share your own battles and victories to inspire him.

- Create a Spiritual Battle Plan: Develop a practical action plan with your son that includes specific scriptures, prayers, and strategies for different situations he might face. Equip him to respond to temptation, fear, or peer pressure with confidence.

- Mentorship and Community: Encourage your son to connect with mentors, youth groups, or Christian communities that will support and strengthen him spiritually. A network of godly influences will reinforce the teachings and practices you have instilled.

Empowering Your Son for a Lifetime of Victory

Equipping your son with spiritual weapons is not a one-time event; it is a continuous process. Your role as a parent is to disciple, encourage, and empower him to fight the good fight of faith. By teaching him to use the full Armor of God, pray with authority, and live a life anchored in Christ, you are preparing him not just for today's battles but for a lifetime of spiritual victory. Remember, the enemy is relentless, but your son, equipped with the right tools, can stand firm and emerge victorious every time.

Celebrating Small Wins and Keeping Hope Alive

When it comes to deliverance and spiritual growth, many parents face a daunting battle: the battle of discouragement. As a parent, you may fervently pray, wage spiritual warfare, and trust God for your son's deliverance. Yet, the journey often seems slow, and progress may appear to be a series of two steps forward, one step back. But it is crucial to understand that every victory, no matter how small, is significant in the Kingdom of God. These small wins are stepping stones that keep hope alive, fuel faith, and ultimately lead to full deliverance.

The Importance of Celebrating Small Wins

In spiritual warfare, the enemy thrives on discouragement. The devil knows that if he can make you feel like nothing is changing, you might abandon the fight. That is why celebrating small victories is not just a good idea—it is a spiritual strategy. Each small win is a testament to God's faithfulness, a beacon of hope, and a reminder that God is at work in your son's life, even if the process is gradual. It is a manifestation of the truth in Zechariah 4:10, which says, "Do not despise these small beginnings, for the Lord rejoices to see the work begin."

Small victories might look like a reduction in negative behavior, a positive shift in attitude, or even a single moment of openness to the Word of God. While these may seem insignificant compared to the full transformation you are praying for, they are evidence of God's hand at work. By celebrating these moments, you acknowledge God's activity in the unseen realms and declare your trust in His perfect timing.

How to Identify and Celebrate Small Wins

Celebrating small wins starts with recognizing them. Often, we are so focused on the ultimate goal that we overlook the signs of progress. Take time to reflect on the changes, however minor, in your son's behavior or spiritual life. Is he more open to conversations about faith? Has he started attending church again, even sporadically? Is there a noticeable change in his mood or willingness to spend time with family? These are all small victories worth celebrating.

Once you identify these small wins, take deliberate steps to celebrate them:

- Speak Life Over Every Progress: The power of words is immense in the spiritual realm. As Proverbs 18:21 states, "Death and life are in the power of the tongue." Use your words to acknowledge and celebrate every positive change you see in your son. Speak it out loud, proclaiming God's ongoing work in his life. Share testimonies of how God is answering your prayers, even if it's a small step. Declare God's promises over him and affirm the progress, no matter how small.

- Thank God Openly and Enthusiastically: When you notice progress, make it a point to praise God openly, both privately and in the presence of your son. Let your gratitude be visible and genuine. This helps to reinforce that God is the source of every good thing and that His hand is actively involved in your son's deliverance journey. Remember, gratitude not only glorifies God but also strengthens your faith and hope, as it aligns your heart with God's perspective.

- Create Rituals of Celebration: Establish a ritual or tradition for acknowledging small wins. This could be a family prayer of thanksgiving, a special dinner, or even a journal where you and your son record the milestones of his journey. These rituals serve as physical reminders of God's faithfulness and create a culture of gratitude and hope within your home. They also provide tangible evidence of God's work, which can be especially encouraging during challenging times.

- Encourage Testimonies and Sharing: Testimonies have power. Revelation 12:11 declares, "They triumphed over him by the blood of the Lamb and by the word of their testimony." Encourage your son to share his experiences, no matter how small, with trusted friends, mentors, or within the church community. When he verbalizes the victories, it helps to build his faith, as well as encourage others who may be going through similar challenges. Testimonies are a powerful weapon against the enemy's attempts to steal hope and joy.

- Practice Spiritual Disciplines Together: Engage in spiritual activities that celebrate God's ongoing work. This could be singing worship songs that declare God's victory, meditating on scriptures that affirm God's promises, or even fasting together as a sign of consecration and dedication. These practices not only honor God but also help to strengthen your son's spiritual foundation, making him more resilient against future attacks.

Staying Focused on the Big Picture

While celebrating small wins is crucial, it is equally important to keep your eyes on the ultimate goal. Understand that deliverance is often a process, not an event. God is not only interested in your son's freedom but also in the formation of his character and the building of his relationship with Him. This means that every small victory is a building block in the greater structure of God's redemptive plan for your son's life.

Remind yourself and your son that God's timing is perfect, and His methods are beyond our understanding. Isaiah 55:8-9 says, "For my thoughts are not your thoughts, neither are your ways my ways," declares the Lord. "As the heavens are higher than the earth, so are my ways higher than your ways and my thoughts than your thoughts." This perspective keeps you grounded in faith, trusting that God knows exactly what He is doing.

Keeping Hope Alive in the Face of Challenges

Deliverance is not always linear. There will be days when progress seems to stall or even regress. During these times, it is critical to keep hope alive. Remember that hope is not just a feeling—it is a choice. Romans 15:13 reminds us, "May the God of hope fill you with all joy and peace as you trust in Him, so that you may overflow with hope by the power of the Holy Spirit." Choose to trust God, even when the evidence is not yet visible.

Encourage your son to develop a resilient hope—a hope that does not waver in the face of setbacks. Teach him to lean on scriptures like Hebrews 11:1, "Now faith is the substance of things hoped for, the evidence of things not seen." Equip him with the understanding that hope is anchored in God's character, not in circumstances.

The Victory Is Already Won

Finally, it is essential to remember that in Christ, the victory is already won. Jesus declared on the cross, "It is finished" (John 19:30), meaning that every power of darkness has already been defeated. Your role as a parent is to enforce this victory through persistent prayer, unwavering faith, and a steadfast commitment to celebrate every evidence of God's grace and power in your son's life.

By celebrating small wins and keeping hope alive, you are not only sustaining your son's deliverance but also building a legacy of faith and perseverance that will stand for generations. As you continue to trust in God, remember that His promise is sure: "He who began a good work in you will carry it on to completion until the day of Christ Jesus" (Philippians 1:6). Keep fighting, keep believing, and keep celebrating—for your son's victory is closer than you think.

Walking in Faith: Trusting God for Total Transformation

In the spiritual journey of praying for deliverance for your teenage son, there comes a point where faith becomes the bedrock of every action, thought, and word. This is the place where you, as a parent, transition from merely praying for your son's freedom to actively walking in faith, believing that the transformation you desire for him is not only possible but is already in motion through the power of God.

Understanding Faith Beyond the Surface

Faith, as the Bible tells us in Hebrews 11:1, is "the substance of things hoped for, the evidence of things not seen." This definition challenges our natural understanding because it asks us to see with spiritual eyes, to believe in what we cannot yet touch, feel, or even comprehend. When praying for your son's deliverance, you must recognize that faith is not passive; it is an active force that shapes reality according to God's promises.

Faith is more than a feeling; it is a conscious decision to trust God wholeheartedly, even when circumstances seem unchanged or contrary to what you are praying for. It is the conviction that God is able to do exceedingly, abundantly above all you could ask or think (Ephesians 3:20). Faith is choosing to see your son not as he is but as God sees him — redeemed, set free, and living victoriously in Christ.

The Dynamics of Walking in Faith

Walking in faith requires a dynamic, multifaceted approach. Here are several components to consider:

1. Confessing God's Promises Over Your Son's Life:
Start by speaking the Word of God over your son daily. Scriptures like Jeremiah 29:11, which affirms God's plans for a future and a hope, or Isaiah 54:13, which declares that all your children will be taught by the Lord, and great will be their peace, should become part of your daily

declarations. Confessing God's promises is not a mere ritual; it is wielding the sword of the Spirit (Ephesians 6:17). Your words have creative power; they align your heart with God's will and release divine intervention in your son's life.

2. Maintaining a Position of Praise:
Praise is a weapon of warfare. It confuses the enemy and magnifies God above every situation. In Acts 16:25-26, Paul and Silas, though bound in prison, began to pray and sing hymns to God. Their praise led to a divine earthquake that broke their chains. In the same way, maintain an attitude of praise. When discouragement comes or when your son's behavior seems to regress, choose to praise God. Praise shifts the atmosphere; it shifts your focus from the problem to the Problem Solver. Remember, it's easy to praise when you see results; the challenge — and the power — comes when you praise in the absence of visible change.

3. Guarding Against Doubt and Fear:
The enemy will attempt to sow seeds of doubt and fear in your heart, making you question whether your prayers are working or if your son will ever change. Recognize these thoughts as spiritual attacks and rebuke them in Jesus' name. Equip yourself with scriptures like 2 Timothy 1:7, which reminds us that God has not given us a spirit of fear but of power, love, and a sound mind. Counter every doubt with the truth of God's Word. Remind yourself that God is faithful and His word will not return void but will accomplish what He desires (Isaiah 55:11).

4. Demonstrating Faith Through Actions:

Walking in faith involves aligning your actions with your prayers. Treat your son with the love and respect that reflects the change you believe God is bringing about in him. Speak to him as though he is already free from the bondages you are praying against. Encourage him, affirm his strengths, and reinforce positive behavior. Be patient, understanding that transformation is a process. Your actions, rooted in faith, will reflect the grace of God and serve as a testimony to your son that God is at work in his life.

5. Creating a Legacy of Faith:

The journey of praying for your son's deliverance is not just about his present condition but about creating a legacy of faith for future generations. Your steadfastness in faith, your commitment to prayer, and your trust in God become a powerful example for your son and others in your family. Remember the story of Hannah in 1 Samuel, who prayed fervently for a son and dedicated him to the Lord even before she saw the promise fulfilled. Her faith set the stage for Samuel, who grew to become a great prophet in Israel. Likewise, your faith and prayers are planting seeds for future spiritual victories, not only for your son but also for generations to come.

Trusting God's Timing and Process

God's timing is often different from our own. It may seem that nothing is happening, but God works in ways that are beyond our understanding.

Trusting God means acknowledging that He knows the perfect time and way to bring about the desired transformation in your son's life. Proverbs 3:5-6 encourages us to "Trust in the Lord with all your heart and lean not on your own understanding; in all your ways submit to him, and he will make your paths straight." Trusting God involves surrender — releasing control and allowing God to work in His time and His way.

Declaring Victory: Moving Forward in Faith

As you walk in faith, continue to declare victory over your son's life. Speak life, hope, and future into his situation. Celebrate every small victory, every sign of progress, knowing that each step forward is a step toward the complete fulfillment of God's promises. Surround yourself with a community of believers who will stand with you in faith, encourage you, and pray with you.

In conclusion, walking in faith is not a passive stance but an active journey of trusting, believing, and declaring God's promises over your son's life. It is standing firm in the assurance that God hears your prayers, sees your tears, and is faithful to bring to completion the good work He has begun in your son (Philippians 1:6). It is believing against all odds, knowing that with God, all things are possible (Matthew 19:26). Your faith, rooted in God's Word and sustained by His Spirit, will pave the way for your son's total transformation and deliverance. Keep believing, keep praying, and keep walking in faith — the victory is already yours in Christ Jesus.

Deliverance Prayers

1. Heavenly Father, I declare in the name of Jesus that my son is set free from every chain that has bound him. I take authority over every spirit that is not of you, and I command it to leave my son's life now. Your Word says whom the Son sets free is free indeed, and I claim that freedom over my son today.

2. Lord Jesus, I ask for divine wisdom and guidance in crafting a daily prayer strategy for my son. May your Holy Spirit guide me in knowing what to pray and when to pray, so that my son remains covered under the shadow of your wings and walks in continuous freedom.

3. In the mighty name of Jesus, I come against any plan, scheme, or agenda of the enemy aimed at my son's life. I cancel it by the power of the blood of Jesus and declare that every weapon formed against him shall not prosper. I stand in the authority given to me by Christ and declare that no evil will befall my son.

4. Father, I pray for the divine protection of my son every day. Surround him with your angels, and place a hedge of fire around him. I declare that no harm, no danger, no attack of the enemy shall come near him, in the name of Jesus.

5. Lord, I lift my son before you each day, asking that you would remind him of your great love and mercy. Let him know that he is your child,

called by your name, and that no power in heaven or on earth can take him from your hand.

6. Almighty God, I take authority in the name of Jesus and build a wall of prayer around my home and family. Let every door and window be covered by the blood of Jesus. May no evil spirit enter this house; let it be a sanctuary of your presence, peace, and protection.

7. I declare my home to be holy ground, consecrated to you, Lord. In the name of Jesus, I cast out every spirit of confusion, strife, and division. I declare that the peace of Christ reigns supreme in this place and that the Holy Spirit is welcomed and honored here.

8. Father, I pray that my family would be unified in you. I come against any spirit of misunderstanding, gossip, or disunity. I declare that my home shall be a house of prayer, love, and understanding, in Jesus' name.

9. Lord, I take authority over every curse, hex, or spell spoken against my home and family. I break every chain of darkness in the name of Jesus and declare that only your Word, your truth, and your promises shall prevail here.

10. In the name of Jesus, I declare my home to be a fortress against all evil. Let the light of your presence be so strong here that darkness has no place. I take authority over every evil influence, and I cast it out by the power of the Holy Spirit.

11. Father God, I pray that you would equip my son with the full armor of God. May he wear the belt of truth, the breastplate of righteousness, the shoes of the gospel of peace, the shield of faith, the helmet of salvation, and wield the sword of the Spirit with authority, in Jesus' name.

12. Lord, I ask that you would give my son a spirit of discernment to recognize the enemy's tactics and schemes. May he always be alert and aware of spiritual battles and respond with wisdom, guided by your Holy Spirit.

13. In the name of Jesus, I declare that my son will stand firm in the faith. He will not be swayed by the lies of the enemy but will hold fast to the truth of your Word, knowing that he is a beloved child of God.

14. Father, I pray that you would give my son the courage and strength to face every challenge. May he never be afraid to stand up for what is right, even when it is difficult. Equip him, Lord, to be a warrior in your kingdom.

15. Lord, I declare that my son will grow in his knowledge of you and your Word. He will hide your Word in his heart so that he will not sin against you. Let your Word be his shield and sword in every battle, in the name of Jesus.

16. Heavenly Father, I thank you for every small victory in my son's life. I celebrate every step he takes toward you, and I declare that these steps will lead to greater victories in his spiritual journey, in Jesus' name.

17. Lord, I pray that you would help me to see and acknowledge the small wins in my son's life. Help me to encourage him daily, to remind him of your goodness, and to keep hope alive in his heart, in the name of Jesus.

18. Father, I take authority over the spirit of discouragement and despair. I declare that my son will not be defeated by setbacks but will rise with renewed strength and faith in you. May every small step forward be a testimony of your power in his life.

19. Lord Jesus, I ask that you keep my son's eyes fixed on you. Let him not grow weary in doing good, knowing that in due season he will reap a great harvest if he does not give up. Keep his hope alive, even in the midst of challenges.

20. I declare in Jesus' name that my son will never lose sight of your promises. Even when things seem difficult, he will hold on to hope and know that you are working all things for his good.

21. Lord, I declare that my son will walk by faith and not by sight. He will trust in your promises, no matter the circumstances, knowing that you are faithful to complete the work you have begun in him.

22. Father, I take authority in the name of Jesus and speak transformation over my son's life. I declare that he will be renewed in mind, body, and spirit and that he will reflect your glory in all he does.

23. Lord Jesus, I pray that my son will trust you fully, even when he doesn't understand. May his faith in you grow stronger each day, knowing that you are his firm foundation.

24. In Jesus' name, I declare that my son will experience total transformation. He will not be conformed to this world but will be transformed by the renewing of his mind, living out your perfect will.

25. Father, I pray that my son's life will be a living testimony of your power and grace. I trust you for his complete deliverance and transformation, and I give you all the glory for the work you are doing in his life.

Appreciation

Thank you for purchasing and reading my book. I am extremely grateful and hope you found value in reading it. Please consider sharing it with friends and family and leaving a review online.

Your feedback and support are always appreciated and allow me to continue doing what I love.

Please go to www.amazon.com
if you'd like to leave a review.

TIMOTHY ATUNNISE's BESTSELLERS

Deliverance & Spiritual Warfare
- Monitoring spirits exposed and defeated.
- Jezebel spirit exposed and defeated.
- Marine spirits exposed and defeated.
- Serpentine spirit exposed and defeated.
- The United Kingdom of darkness exposed & defeated.
- Ahithophel Spirit Unmasked
- Kundalini Spirit Unmasked
- Prophetic warfare: Unleashing supernatural power in warfare.
- The time is now: A guide to overcoming marital delay.
- Earth moving prayers: Pray until miracles happen.
- I must win this battle: Expanded edition.
- I must my financial battle
- Essential prayers
- Open heavens: Unlocking divine blessings and breakthroughs.
- This battle ends now.
- Breaking the unbreakable
- Reversing evil handwriting
- I must win this battle - French edition.
- I must win this battle - Spanish edition.
- Ammunition for spiritual warfare
- Reversing the Irreversible
- Let there be a change.

- Total Deliverance: Volume 1
- 21 days prayer for total breakthroughs
- Warrior Mom: Defending your children in the court of heaven.
- The Power of Fathers' prayer
- Overcoming afflictions in the workplace
- The art of spiritual vision casting
- Thriving beyond letdowns: Overcoming constant disappointments
- The Anointed Intercessor: A Prayer Warrior's Calling
- Prayers of the Midnight Warriors
- Spiritual Mapping 101: A Beginner's Guide
- Deliverance from Satanic Dreams and Nightmares
- Inherited battles, victorious lives: Power to conquer ancestral strongholds and liberate your family's destiny.
- From bondage to breakthrough
- Learn to choose your battles.
- Total deliverance from spirit spouse
- Last minute miracles
- Unshackled
- Overcoming spiritual bullying & intimidation
- The heavenly advocate's handbook
- Breaking ungodly soul-ties
- It is finished
- Overcoming demonic instruments of derailment
- Pursue, overtake, and recover
- Power of midnight praise – Book 1
- Power of midnight praise – Book 2

- Defeating witchcraft attacks
- Dangerous enemies, dangerous prayers
- Rising from the dungeon of darkness
- Back to Sender Prayers
- Reclaiming your mind
- Identifying & Dismantling Evil Altars
- Overcoming the Invisible Assault
- Deliverance from Star Hunters
- The Devil's Playbook Exposed

Deliverance from Witchcraft Attacks
- Deliverance from Enchantment & Black Magic
- Rise above the curse: An empowering guide to overcome witchcraft attacks.
- Breaking the Family Curse: Unraveling the Past for a Brighter Future and Transform Your Family Legacy
- Breaking Chains of Rejection: A personal deliverance manual

Weapons of Warfare
- The Name of Jesus: The unstoppable weapon of warfare
- Praise and Worship: Potent weapons of warfare
- Blood of Jesus: The ultimate weapon
- The Word of God as a weapon: A double-edged sword to bring transformation and unparallel victory in spiritual warfare.
- Praying with Power: The warrior's guide to weapon of dynamic warfare prayer

- The weapon of prophetic dreams
- Praying in tongues of heaven
- Waging war through fasting: The incontestable weapon of spiritual warfare
- The fire of God's presence: A weapon of unparallel strength & potency
- The Word of Testimony – A stealth weapon of spiritual warfare
- Angelic assistance in spiritual warfare
- The art of spiritual discernment: Your warfare advantage

Prayer Ministry
- Intercessory prayer
- Corporate prayer
- Prevailing prayer
- Imprecatory prayer
- Healing through prayer & fasting
- The prayer leader's handbook
- How to build a successful global prayer network
- Overcoming Spiritual Dryness
- Hearing & recognizing the voice of God
- When God's says NO and prayers go unanswered

Power of Anointing
- The power of anointing for success: Partnering with God in extraordinary moments for great success
- The Power of Anointing for Generational Wealth

- Anointing for Disconnection

Holy Spirit
- Holy Spirit my prayer partner

14 Days Prayer & Fasting Series
- 14 Days prayer to break evil patterns.
- 14 days prayer against delay and stagnation
- 14 days prayer for a new beginning
- 14 days prayer for deliverance from demonic attacks
- 14 days prayer for total healing
- 14 days prayer for deliverance from rejection and hatred
- 14 days prayer for healing the foundations
- 14 days prayer for breaking curses and evil covenants
- 14 days prayer for uncommon miracles
- 14 days prayer for restoration and total recovery
- 14 days prayer: It's time for a change
- 14 days prayer for deliverance from witchcraft attacks
- 14 days prayer for accelerated promotion
- 14 days prayer for deliverance from generational problems
- 14 days prayer for supernatural supply
- 14 days prayer to God's will for your life
- 14 days prayer for Mountaintop Experience
- 14 days prayer for home, family and marriage restoration
- 14 days prayer to overcome stubborn situations.
- 14 days prayer for restoration of stolen destiny

- 14 days prayer for financial breakthroughs
- 14 Days Prayer for Extraordinary Success & Great Achievements
- 14 Days prayer against failure at the edge of success
- 14 Days prayer for breaking the curse of almost
- 14 Days prayer for restoration of wasted years & efforts

7 Days Prayer & Fasting Series
- Breaking the chains of delay & waiting
- My story must change.

Personal Finances
- The art of utility bills negotiation
- From strapped to successful: Unlocking financial freedom beyond Paycheck to paycheck
- Escape the rat race: How to retire in five years or less.
- Mastering mean reversion: A guide to profitable trading, so simple a 10-year-old can understand
- Breaking the chains of debt
- Poverty is not an option
- Building seven streams of income

Bible Study
- The King is coming
- Seven judgments of the Bible
- The miracle of Jesus Christ
- The book of Exodus

- Lost and found: The house of Israel
- The parables of Jesus Christ
- Erased by the Cross

Fiction
- The merchant's legacy: A tale of faith and family
- A world unraptured: Brink of oblivion
- Gone: A chronicle of chaos
- The Sunshine Country

Family Counseling
- Healing whispers: Biblical comfort and healing for men after miscarriage

Leadership/Business
- The most intelligent woman: A woman's guide to outsmarting any room at any level
- Thriving in the unknown: Preparing children for careers that don't exist yet.
- Communication breakthrough: Cultivating deep connections through active listening.
- Overcoming Procrastination
- Raising Christian Leaders: A Parent's Guide

Spiritual Growth

- Divine Intimacy: Embracing the Transformative Power of Intimate Communion to Discover Profound Connection and Fulfillment
- 7 Steps to Receiving a Miracle
- 7 Simple Secrets to Consistent Answered Prayers
- The art of forgiving the unforgettable
- Grace Unleashed
- Worship without Love

Prophetic Books
- Walking in prophetic anointing
- Walking in prophetic authority
- Embracing the prophetic call

Personal Growth
- Divine masterpiece
- God has your back
- How to make wise decisions
- The danger of over-familiarity with God

Theology/Ministry
- Laughing Pulpit: Using humor to enhance preaching.
- Prophecies and Visions
- Understanding the Pentateuch
- Typology
- The Seven Dispensations

Family Deliverance Series
- Deliverance Prayer for Adult Children
- Deliverance Prayer for Teenage Daughter
- Deliverance Prayer for Teenage Son

Parenting/Relationship
- Embracing metamorphosis: Nurturing teenage girls' remarkable journey into adulthood

Mental Health
- The power of inner healing

Marriage/Family
- The conscious husband: Mastering active listening in marriage.
- The conscious wife: Nurturing relationship with awareness, building a perfect and flourishing family.
- Conscious parenting: Mastering active listening to your children.
- From cradle to consciousness: Guiding your child's awareness
- The 'Not Tonight' syndrome: Overcoming false excuses in marital intimacy.
- 12 Practical steps to making your marriage heaven on earth
- Couple's workshop
- Sacred Intimacy

End-Times
- Dawn of eternity: Unraveling the rapture of the saints

- Signs of the end-times: Deciphering prophecies in a race against time
- The rise of the Antichrist: Unveiling the beast and the prophecies

The King is Coming
- The Departure
- Understanding the Judgment Seat of Christ
- Believers' Rewards
- Zion's Final Hour
- Tribulation
- The Great Tribulation
- The Seventy Weeks of Daniel
- The Marriage Supper of the Lamb
- The Battle of Armageddon
- Countdown to the Kingdom
- The Millennial Kingdom
- The Final Chapter

Short eBooks
- Unleash the fury.
- Walking on water
- Unlonely

Printed in Great Britain
by Amazon